RETREAT, HELL!
We Just Got Here!

'They looked larger than ordinary men; their tall, straight figures were
in vivid contrast to the under-sized armies of pale recruits to which we
had grown accustomed. At first I thought their spruce, clean uniforms
were those of officers, yet obviously they could not be officers, for there
were too many of them; they seemed, as it were, Tommies in heaven.
Had yet another regiment been conjured out of our depleted Dominions?
I wondered, watching them move with such rhythm, such dignity,
such serene consciousness of self respect...

Then I heard an excited exclamation from a group of Sisters behind me.
"Look! Look! Here are the Americans!"'

Vera Brittain, *Testament of Youth*

RETREAT, HELL!
We Just Got Here!

The American Expeditionary Force in France 1917-1918

MARTIN MARIX EVANS

OSPREY
MILITARY

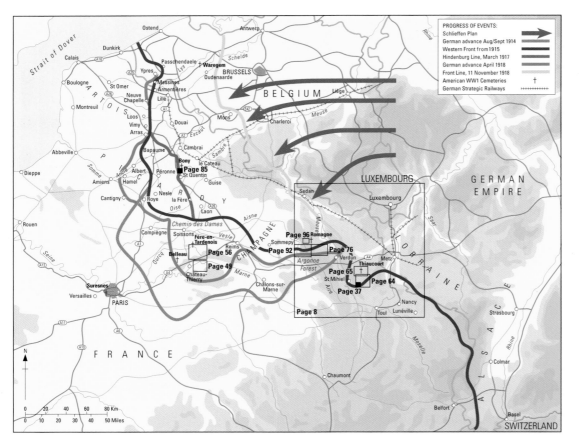

Left **The Western Front, 1914-18.** Major modern roads are shown, and the coverage of the more detailed maps included in the text is shown together with the number of the relevant page.

DEDICATION

To my father, Jean-Paul, who gave me the original idea for this book, my American relatives and my American brothers, one, Robin, a brother by birth and the other, Jim, a brother in spirit. And, as always, to my wife and helper, Gillian.

ISBN 1 85532 777 5

Editors: Sharon van der Merwe/Conor Kilgallon
Design: The Black Spot
Cartography by The Map Studio, courtesy Pitkin Unichrome Ltd.

Filmset in Singapore by pica Ltd.
Printed through World Print Ltd., Hong Kong

98 99 00 01 02   10 9 8 7 6 5 4 3 2 1

For a catalogue of all books published by Osprey Military please write to:
The Marketing Manager, Osprey Publishing Ltd, PO Box 140, Wellingborough, Northants NN8 4ZA

ACKNOWLEDGEMENTS

The constructive, courteous and patient assistance of the staff of the US Army Military History Institute, Carlisle, Pennsylvania, is most gratefully acknowledged, and in particular, that of Dr Richard Sommers, David Keogh, John Slonaker, Michael Winey and Randy Hackenburg. For helping to guide me to Carlisle in the first place and for local knowledge, I must thank John Kallmann and Gary Mead. I have again been fortunate in benefiting from the work of Toby Buchan on the script and thank him most sincerely.

Most of the black and white photographs are from the archives of the US Army Military History Institute (USAMHI); where these are Army Signal Corps (ASC) pictures the identification number, if known, is given. Where the photograph comes from the USAMHI World War I Survey, the number of the division, the family name, given name and rank of the service person under whom it is filed are given, again if known. Other black and white photographs are from the Tank Museum, Bovington, Dorset (TM), the Historial de la Grande Guerre, PÇronne (HGG) and the Imperial War Museum, London (IWM); and their identification numbers are given. The colour photographs are by the author. The sources of maps are similarly acknowledged, using the initials noted above. Ordnance Survey maps are Crown Copyright. The photograph used on the half-title page is of a sculpture on the door of the chapel at St-Mihiel Cemetery (MFME Yp/Ar 5/E) and the picture on the title page is from the collection of Major William Sweeney, VI Corps (USAMHI/WWI).

The majority of the eyewitness accounts quoted are from original documents and are introduced with the name of the USAMHI World War I Survey file from which they come. They have been quoted as written, and without the distracting insertion of the word 'sic'. Other quotations are from books published by the person quoted, with the exception of the words of Paul Shaffer, which are taken from The Doughboys by Laurence Stallings, George Patton, from The Pattons by Robert Patton, and Captain Harry S. Truman, which come from A Stillness Heard Round the World by Stanley Weintraub. All these books are listed in the bibliography. The Vera Brittain quotation from Testament of Youth is included with the permission of her literary executors and Victor Gollancz, publishers and the John Thomason extracts with the permission of Simon & Schuster. At the time of going to press the literary executors of certain authors have not been traced and the author will be grateful for any information as to their identity and whereabouts.

CONTENTS

ON THE SIDELINES

Leopold Lojka was not told. His employer, Count Franz Harrach, had lent his car to his friend, the Archduke Franz Ferdinand, to make a visit to Sarajevo and, of course, driver Lojka was included in the loan. Now, in a turbulent province of the Austro–Hungarian Empire, he had just managed to avoid a bomb thrown at his august passengers and was attempting to get them out of town. If only they had told him the route had been changed! Wrong way? Lojka halted the car and struggled to back up, but as he did so a young man rushed forward and fired his Browning pistol twice. The Archduke and his wife were fatally injured. On this Sunday, 28 June 1914, Gavrilo Princip, the Serbian assassin, had set in motion a chain of events that would leave widows and orphans in every continent of the globe.

The Austrians held the Serbs responsible for the outrage and attempted to impose terms on them which could not be accepted. Most significantly, the Austrians called for the absorption of Serbia. The Russians supported the Serbs, threatening the Austro-Hungarian Empire in a way that the Germans were only too happy to declare intolerable. The German counter-threat to Russia made it imperative for France to become

Above **Kaiser Wilhelm II and the German Chief of Staff in 1914, General Helmuth von Moltke, nephew of the architect of France's defeat in the Franco-Prussian War of 1870, General Helmuth, Count von Moltke.** (IWM Q91832)

involved, and thus the web of treaties that was believed to offer stability through a balance of power entrapped them all. What was more, the Germans faced the prospect of war on two fronts, in the east against Russia

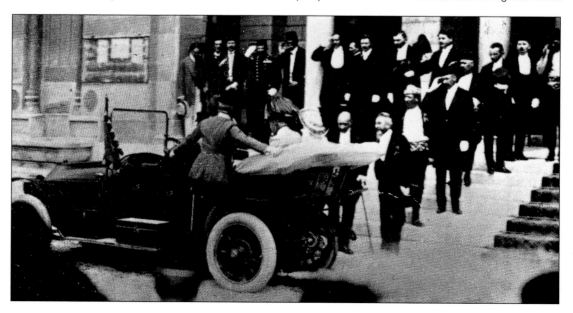

Right **Archduke Franz Ferdinand leaves the reception in Sarajevo in a fury, insulted by an attempt to kill him and his wife with a bomb.** (IWM Q91848)

and in the west against France. This had been foreseen. Colonel-General Count Alfred von Schlieffen, Chief of the German General Staff from 1891 to 1905, devised a plan to strike at France through the Netherlands and Belgium, avoiding the defences and fortified towns that protected her eastern border from Verdun to Belfort. That this meant violating the neutrality of Belgium, a status Germany herself had guaranteed, was ignored. Schlieffen's successor, Colonel-General Helmuth von Moltke, modified the plan so as to bypass the Netherlands and assumed that the Belgians would either capitulate or offer only token resistance. Great Britain's status as a guarantor of Belgian neutrality was considered irrelevant, as the whole operation was to be completed in six weeks, too fast for Britain to react even if she chose to do so.

The French, too, had a plan. In 1911 General Michel, the Commander-in-Chief designate in the event of war, had proposed a plan based on the defence of a line from Antwerp to Namur and from there to Verdun. A response, in fact, to the thinking that informed the Schlieffen Plan. It was treated with scorn. It lacked the spirit of attack at all costs – *attaque à outrance* – to which the French were dedicated. Michel was ousted and his job was combined with that of Chief of the General Staff. General Joseph Joffre was chosen to fill the post and under his control a new plan, Plan XVII, was devised. The French would strike from positions of strength in the east of their country, through the provinces of Alsace and Lorraine which had been lost to Prussia in the Franco-Prussian War of 1870. This plan would take the battle to the German heartland.

The forces at the disposal of the main participants were huge. Germany, Austria, France and Russia all conscripted men for compulsory military service, with Germany the keenest of all. Indeed, German militarism had so alarmed the United States that in 1913 President Woodrow Wilson had sent Colonel Edward M. House to Europe to attempt to calm the situation and to encourage the complacent British to take it seriously. Germany had a peacetime regular army of 880,000 men and Austria-Hungary 480,000. They were capable of mobilising, by drawing in reservists, 4,500,000 and 2,000,000 respectively. Russia had a peacetime strength of 1,400,000 and a mobilised manpower of 4,500,000, though of very doubtful quality. France maintained a force of 823,250 in peacetime and could mobilise 3,781,000. Compared to these massive numbers, the forces of the other nations were tiny. Serbia could call on 459,500 but had only 30,000 men under arms in peace, while Belgium's peacetime force of 48,000 could, given time, be expanded to just 217,000. Britain's Regular Army of 255,000 was spread across her worldwide empire, but only 120,000 men were serving in

Europe, and the fully mobilised strength of all her troops came to just 713,500. In April 1917, when the USA declared war, the American regular troops numbered 127,588 and the army's reserve, the National Guard, 80,436.

The diplomatic activity of July 1914 was frantic. The Germans pressured the Austrians to act against Serbia, but they were reluctant to do so. Indeed, their envoy to Sarajevo reported on 13 July that there was no evidence to show that the Serbs were implicated in the assassination. None the less, the Austrian Council of State decided that, once the French state visit to Russia was over on 23 July, an ultimatum would be sent to the Serbs. The note was duly sent; it demanded a reply within 48 hours. Prince Alexander of Serbia appealed to the Tsar for Russian help, and the British Foreign Minister, Sir Edward Grey, proposed mediation. In spite of a humiliatingly conciliatory response from Serbia, Austria declared war on her on Tuesday 28 July. With ghastly inevitability Russia mobilised and a succession of ultimatums and declarations of war followed.

From his country home in Surrey, located 20 miles south-west of London, the Ambassador of the United States of America to the Court of St James, Walter H. Page, wrote to his President, Woodrow Wilson, on Sunday 2 August.

The Grand Smash is come. Last night the German Ambassador at St Petersburg handed the Russian Government a declaration of war... It is reported in London today that the Germans have invaded Luxemburg and France... Colonel Squier [the American Military Attaché]... sees no way for England to keep out of it.

The diplomatic activity of July 1914 was frantic.

On 4 August, the Germans crossed the Belgian border...

On 4 August, the Germans crossed the Belgian border seven hours before the British ultimatum, which had forbidden them to do so, ran out. Britain declared war on Germany.

Ambassador Page wrote to the President the following Sunday.

God save us! What a week it has been! ... Then came the declaration of war, most dramatically... An indescribable crowd so blocked the streets about the Admiralty, the War Office and the Foreign Office that I had to drive in my car by other streets to get home... The next day the German Embassy was turned over to me... [In wartime, the embassies of belligerents are looked after by neutral powers,

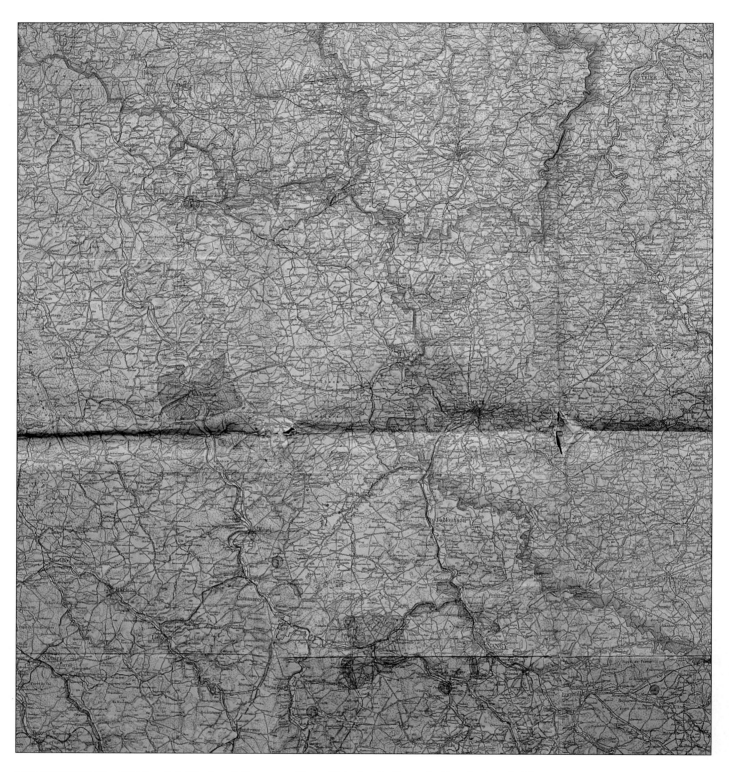

A pre-war German map of the French fortifications in the east, facing the border which is marked in purple. The fortifications planned by General Séré de Rivières in 1875 are shown with red dots and major areas of defence with red shading, forming three sides of a rectangle around the Woevre Plain. As a bastion against invasion it worked, but as a jump-off for attack in 1914 it was a failure. St-Mihiel, on the River Meuse, is halfway between the strongpoints of Verdun and Toul, and the Meuse-Argonne region lies west and north-west of Verdun. (Coll. Brian Kibby)

Above **French soldiers man a machine-gun in defence of Fort Vaux on the hills above Verdun.** (MFME Hist/Somme 1/32. HGG)

as their staffs return to their own countries.] Then came the crowds of frightened Germans, afraid they would be arrested... Every day Germans are arrested on suspicion; and several of them have committed suicide... A United States Senator telegraphs me: 'Send my wife and daughter home on the first ship.' Ladies and gentlemen filled the steerage of that ship – not a bunk left; and his wife and daughter are found three days later sitting in a swell hotel waiting for me to bring them stateroom tickets on a silver tray!... Six American preachers pass a resolution unanimously 'urging our Ambassador to telegraph our beloved, peace-loving President to stop this awful war'; and they come with simple solemnity to present their resolution.

THE FORMATION OF THE WESTERN FRONT

The French and the Germans at once put their plans into action. From Belfort a thrust through the Vosges took the French as far as Mulhouse with little resistance. Within days they were thrown back by reinforcements that the Germans had hurried down from Strasbourg. In the north the attempted advance north-east of Nancy broke against the fortifications of Morhange and Sarrebourg, and the garrison of Metz moved against the left flank of the French attack. Plan XVII was failing; a vicious confrontation would fix this front in a position which, three years later, the Americans would find had altered little.

In Belgium the forts protecting the city of Liège refused to allow the invaders to pass unopposed. To their surprise the Germans found they had to fight and, throwing themselves prodigally against the fortifications, to die. Heavy guns soon overcame the gallant Belgian resistance, but, although opposed by only small forces of Belgians, French and British, the Schlieffen Plan unfolded not only too slowly, but also in the wrong place. The intended envelopment of Paris was not achieved and the Germans were stopped on the River Marne to the east of the city. For a time a great open

Above **A French working party on the Somme front. The chalky soil indicated with complete clarity the locations of innumerable trenches. That they are wearing steel helmets shows that this picture was made after April 1915.** (MFME Hist/Somme 2/24. HGG)

Below **Belts of barbed wire, in some places five or six hundred yards deep, lay in wait for the Allied infantry.** (TM)

Almost the whole of Belgium and a great part of France were in German hands.

Right **Men of the 18th Infantry, US 1st Division, in a shell hole at Froissey, 16 May 1918, with a French Hotchkiss machine-gun.** (USAMHI/ASC 13166) [1/33]

Below **Heavy and light Maxim machine-guns, and a 77-mm field gun, captured from the Germans by the 26th Division, August 1918.** (USAMHI/ASC) [6/27]

space existed between Paris and Calais with few forces of either side to contest the ground. This led to a series of attempted flanking movements by the opposing armies, afterwards described as 'the race to the sea'. By the valiant and desperate action known as the First Battle of Ypres, the British, French and Belgians prevented the Germans taking the vital ports of Dunkirk and Calais on the coast of the English Channel. As the troops dug in, each side unable either to overrun or outflank the other, the Western Front had formed. It ran in a line from the south-eastern corner of Belgium, south across Artois and Picardy towards Paris, then east, north of Soissons and Reims, through Champagne and the Argonne to Verdun and away south-east, round the salient of St-Mihiel and east of Nancy and Belfort to the Swiss border. Almost the whole of Belgium and a great part of France, including the industrial north with three-quarters of her iron and coal industries, were in German hands. Advocates of immediate peace, then

and now, appear to have ignored the territorial and economic impact of German success.

As the Western Front formed in the fall of 1914, Ambassador Page wrote to his son enclosing a letter, a copy of which was sent to the President, dated 25 September 1914 and purportedly written by a woman born in England who had lived many years with her German husband in Bremen. It had been sent to an old friend in Britain. Page observed that it demonstrated the extent to which ordinary people in Germany were fooling themselves. Having expressed the German contempt for all things British, it included the following passage.

England is, after all, only a stepping stone. From Liverpool, Queenstown [now Cobh], Glasgow, Belfast, we shall reach out across the ocean. I firmly believe that within a year Germany will have seized the new [Panama] Canal and proclaimed its defiance of the Monroe Doctrine [which stated that European powers should not interfere in America's affairs]. We have six million Germans in the United States, and the Irish-Americans behind them... By our possession of the entire Western European seaboard America can find no outlet for its products except by our favour. Her finance is in German hands, her commercial capitals, New York and Chicago, are in reality German cities.

TRENCH WARFARE AND TECHNOLOGY

The war of movement, a war for which the generals were prepared and in which they were experienced, ceased as the opposing armies dug in. Technical advances had created the stalemate. Although the immediate practical use of new weapons was easily grasped, the development of appropriate tactics and of yet newer weapons to counter the power at the enemy's disposal took a long time. The cost, in human lives, of the learning process was immense. At the outbreak of war, two of these new weapons were available, the machine-gun and modern artillery, and a new defensive device was to hand, barbed wire. Two of the three were American innovations.

Hiram Maxim was an American, though later a naturalised British citizen. In the late 19th century he devised a gun that used the recoil automatically to eject the spent cartridge, load a new round, recock the weapon and fire once more. The four operations being all but simultaneous, thus giving a very high rate of fire. The European powers, intent on the arms race, took up the concept with enthusiasm. The British version was the Vickers-Maxim, the German the Maxim and the French the St-Étienne. All were theoretically capable of firing 500-600 rifle-calibre rounds per minute, though even water-cooling could not prevent overheating should such rates be attempted. Machine-gunners were therefore trained to fire in bursts. The new guns were heavy weapons, the Maxim weighing 115 pounds (52kg) and the lighter Vickers 68 pounds (31kg), and had to be mounted on tripods and usually moved on light carriages or sleds. The French company, Hotchkiss, founded by an American, developed a gas-powered, air-cooled gun that was somewhat lighter. For defensive fire against both infantry and cavalry these machine guns were particularly potent.

In 1911, the American Colonel Isaac Newton Lewis offered his government a machine-gun of his own invention that was even lighter, the 25-pound, gas-operated, drum-fed, air-cooled Lewis, which used the same .303 ammunition as the British Lee-Enfield rifle and the Vickers. The US Government turned it down, and Lewis eventually had it produced by the Belgian FN company and, later, in Britain. It was not until the weapon came into service with the British, late in 1915, that the US Government deemed it worthy of attention. After America entered the war in 1917, however, the US Army opted for the Browning .30 automatic rifle as its light machine-gun, although only a prototype existed and the weapons were not expected to be available in the field before April 1918. In the meantime US troops used the Lewis. The German light machine-gun was the Maxim 08/15, water-cooled, and heavier at 31 pounds.

Private Donald D. Kyler, G Company, 2nd Battalion, 16th Infantry Regiment, US 1st Division, of Elkhart, Indiana, later recalled:

We were issued one French chauchat machine rifle to each squad... [It] weighed over 20 pounds and was recoil operated. Ammunition was supplied to it in spring-loaded magazines... [which] held 20 rounds of French rifle cartridges. One gun could shoot more shots than all the rest of the squad combined for short periods... But it was not accurate... was too heavy, too clumsy to aim and in general not effective except against very close concentrated targets. About a year later [i.e. July 1918] those rifles were replaced by American-made Browning machine rifles, which were an improvement.

Above **French 155-mm long-range guns on the Somme front, 1916.** (MFME Hist/Somme 2/16. HGG)

Left **A Lewis gun mounted as an anti-aircraft weapon in New Zealand trenches at Gommecourt, 10 August 1918.** (TM 5086/E5)

The Browning weapon was lighter than the chauchat, with an adjustable rate of fire, could be shot singly or in short bursts, and used our rifle cartridges. The regular magazine held 20 rounds, but magazines were available that held 40 rounds. It was a good weapon, but with the same limitations as the chauchat and had a few faults of its own. One was

that it fired too fast on automatic, resulting in the loss of very effective aim. Another was that of frequent jams in the mechanism... A little sand or mud getting into the chamber or magazine could cause a malfunction. Also, the gas port sometimes became clogged, causing failure of the extraction and ejection mechanism, which was gas operated.

Kyler goes on to express the view that 'machine rifles' were not suited to use in units intended to be mobile, though self-loading rifles were. Their inaccuracy, unreliability and greed for ammunition counted against them. Medium machine-guns like the Vickers, on the other hand, he valued for their long-range harassing firepower when used in support of infantry attacks, firing over the heads of the advancing troops. It is interesting that his analysis is entirely related to the use of weapons in attack, a point of view typical of the Americans who had small experience of the long misery of trench warfare.

Artillery development in the 25 years preceding the war had also been dramatic, providing the gunners with breech-loading field guns, howitzers and immense rail-mounted weapons of unprecedented power, range and accuracy. Such was the impression of might imposed by these weapons that excessive reliance was placed upon them for the destruction of enemy defences. As the British were to learn on the Somme, their use against another American invention, barbed wire, was limited by the effectiveness of their shells and the state of the terrain - the wrong choice of shell, inadequate fuses or soft mud could render them harmless.

The air had not yet become a battle area in 1914. Balloons and aircraft were used for observation and reconnaissance; combat machines were yet to come. Armoured cars roamed open country in the early weeks of the war, but could not operate in the context of trench warfare. It was not until 1916 that the first

tanks were seen in battle, armoured landships running on caterpillar tracks and capable of crossing trenches in the face of machine-gun fire. They gave the first hope of recovering movement in this static war, but were mechanically unreliable as well as too lightly armoured to survive shellfire. The lozenge-shaped British heavy tanks weighed 28 tons and their puny 105-horsepower engines pushed them along at a mere half a mile per hour off road. Improved versions swiftly followed, with bigger engines, heavier armour and, eventually, even radio communication. However, they remained primitive and liable to bog down in broken ground and mud – precisely the sort of terrain created by artillery barrages laid down by their own side. French efforts went mainly into the development of the Renault 6.4-ton light tank, a two-man vehicle which gave its commander so many tasks that effectiveness was compromised. He had to navigate, observe, fire the 37-mm gun and direct the driver, who was fully occupied with the challenge of controlling the vehicle's movements. When used in numbers in open country and firm ground conditions, however, the Renaults were successful. The three-man British Whippet 14-ton medium tank was a nimble vehicle which enjoyed even greater success, whereas the French Schneider, of similar weight, was a clumsy, flawed design even though it packed a mighty 75-mm gun and two machine-guns. The Germans recovered British tanks abandoned after they had bogged down, or which were damaged but reparable, and also built a monster 30-ton iron tortoise, the A7V Sturmpanzerwagen. It bristled with six machine-guns and a 57-mm gun, but was unmanoeuvrable and top-heavy, with a tendency to fall ignominiously on its side. In the two years between their first use and the end of the war the technical development of the tank proceeded at a remarkable pace, but the principal difficulty for the major combatants was building enough machines. Although the Allies put plans in hand to manufacture them in the USA only two tanks, Renaults, had been shipped to Europe by the end of the war.

The trenches themselves became more complex and sophisticated as time went on. The first trivial scrapes in the dirt became deep cuttings in which a man could walk upright unobserved, and the art of fortification, so deeply studied over the last two centuries, blossomed once more. The Germans were determined to hold what territory they had gained. To this end, they generously spent both energy and materials to construct complex trench systems and deep dugout shelters designed to ensure the survival of defenders subjected to artillery bombardment, and to provide optimum positions from which to repel infantry attacks. The French and British, on the other hand, were initially dedicated to ejecting the invader and saw their positions as starting points for the required attack, consequently building light, supposedly temporary, trench systems. As the war drew on their trenches, too, became complex arrangements of front and supporting lines, communication trenches and dugouts.

THE MERCANTILE WAR

The battles of 1914 had exacted a terrible toll upon the French, who had nearly a million men killed, wounded or made prisoner by the end of the year. The British had been able to send an expeditionary force of only 103,700 men and had suffered 95,500 casualties in the same period. The British Regular Army was all but wiped out. Belgian losses numbered 50,000. More than a third of Moltke's German Field Army, which numbered around one and a half million men, was lost.

Although the response in Britain to the appeal for volunteers was huge – two and a half million would enlist by the end of 1915 – the problem was to train them as soldiers. Reinforcements were drawn from reservists, the Territorial Force (the equivalent of the American National Guard) and from the countries of the Empire. The actions undertaken against the

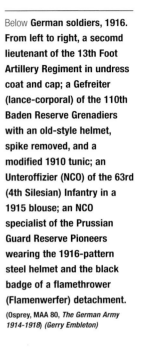

Below **German soldiers, 1916. From left to right, a secomd lieutenant of the 13th Foot Artillery Regiment in undress coat and cap; a Gefreiter (lance-corporal) of the 110th Baden Reserve Grenadiers with an old-style helmet, spike removed, and a modified 1910 tunic; an Unteroffizier (NCO) of the 63rd (4th Silesian) Infantry in a 1915 blouse; an NCO specialist of the Prussian Guard Reserve Pioneers wearing the 1916-pattern steel helmet and the black badge of a flamethrower (Flamenwerfer) detachment.** (Osprey, MAA 80, *The German Army 1914-1918*) *(Gerry Embleton)*

Germans were, therefore, limited in scope and largely unsuccessful. The Germans were active mainly on the Eastern Front against Russia, but they did make an attack on the Belgians, French and British (including the Canadians) in the Ypres Salient. There, on 22 April 1915, they made the first use of poison gas in warfare. In neutral America this was seen as a barbaric action, confirming the German atrocities reported during the invasion of Belgium. The greatest impact on the United States, however, came from actions at sea.

Britain's concern was to prevent supplies reaching Germany. This included deploying the Royal Navy to stop and search neutral shipping and seize goods deemed contraband. This practice interfered with American business when US ships were searched. It was a complex area of international law and much was said by both sides – Ambassador Page was a busy man. In January 1915 an American, one Mr Breitung, purchased a German merchantman, the *Dacia*, then lying at Port Arthur, Texas, with the intention of sending her to Germany with a load of cotton. A serious dispute with Britain was certain as the vessel would surely be seized. The elegant solution was to have her seized by the French with whom, as a legacy of France's support and friendship dating back to the War of Independence, the Americans were sympathetic.

Equally, Germany was determined to deny Britain imports by sea but, lacking a surface fleet powerful enough to defeat the Royal Navy, declared that from 4 February 1915 the waters around Britain and Ireland would be considered part of the war zone within which her U-boats would destroy enemy merchant shipping. Most significantly, the ships of neutrals would also be at risk in the war zone. Since this also put the lives of neutrals at risk, America protested strongly. On 1 May the American tanker SS *Gulflight* was torpedoed off the Scilly Isles at the western end of the English Channel and three US citizens died. Six days later the Cunard liner RMS *Lusitania* was torpedoed off the south coast of Ireland. She sank in a mere 20 minutes with the loss of 1,198 people, including 124 Americans and 94 children.

Although the Germans claimed the liner had been carrying munitions and was armed – and thus a legitimate target – a wave of revulsion swept across America. Colonel House, in England at the time, was sure the President would declare war. A day or two later House was walking in London's Piccadilly and saw, to his dismay, a newspaper vendor's sign: '"We are too proud to fight" – Woodrow Wilson.'

American protests to Germany met with evasive replies, but in July an undertaking was given to allow US vessels to pass unhindered. The value of this was, however, undermined by the deaths of two more Americans in the sinking of the British ship *Arabic* in August. The tide of opinion on the other side of the Atlantic began to turn against Germany.

THE KILLING FIELDS

On 21 February 1916 General Erich von Falkenhayn, Chief of the German General Staff (he had succeeded Moltke after the German defeat on the Marne in September 1914), unleashed a massive assault on the forts on the hills above the fortified French city of Verdun. The concentration of artillery was unprecedented, 1,400 guns, many of them huge 'siege' howitzers, were turned on the defenders. Falkenhayn knew that the French regarded attack as the best form of defence. With this in mind, he attempted to entrap the French into destroying themselves in the battle for a place regarded in France as of overwhelming symbolic importance. This achieved, he would be able to defeat the British in their turn. What Falkenhayn did not know was that Joffre regarded the Verdun forts as of little strategic value and had therefore reduced the garrisons to token forces. In spite of the heroic defence made by

Above, left **September 1916: A British Mark I moves up in the Somme area for the first tank action in history.** (TM54/E3)

Above **A French Schneider on manoeuvres near Breteuil, 11 May 1918.** (USAMHI/ASC 13105) [3/5,6]

the unfortunate remainder, the Germans overcame the forts of Douaumont and Vaux and found themselves drawn in to a close encounter which, by the end of March, would cost them 81,000 casualties to the 89,000 suffered by the French. The battle continued throughout the summer. By the end of October Fort Douaumont was back in French hands and Fort Vaux was regained early in November. When attacks ceased on 18 December, 66 French divisions had been in action at Verdun, suffering losses – killed, wounded, missing or captured – of 362,000 men, while the 42 German divisions there had lost 336,800.

With the French engaged at Verdun, the Commander-in-Chief of the British Expeditionary Force, General Sir Douglas Haig, came under increasing pressure to mount an attack in the west to dilute the German strength. In Britain, the masses of volunteers were approaching readiness for battle, but were still untested, while the supply of artillery and ammunition fell well short of what was desirable in order to strike a major blow. Nevertheless, on 1 July 1916 the British and French launched a huge assault on German lines in the valley of the River Somme. The events of that first day of what, in the end, would be a series of offensives lasting four and a half months still awaken deep emotions in British hearts. The intensive artillery bombardment, though it lasted for a week, did not cut the enemy's barbed wire in many places, and it failed to smash the deep underground bunkers built by the Germans in the malleable chalk of the gently rolling landscape. The machine-gunners scrambled up to man their front-line trenches, mount their weapons and cut down the advancing lines of British troops. Rockets rose in the air to call down artillery fire on pre-targeted positions through which the attackers had to pass. The slaughter was immense. On that day 19,240 British soldiers died, 35,493 were wounded, 2,152 were missing and 585 were taken prisoner. This remains the highest casualty total suffered by the British Army in a single day.

The plan had been to break through the German lines and strike swiftly with cavalry towards Bapaume, allowing the infantry to pour into the gap and roll up the enemy line northwards and southwards. When the battle spluttered to a halt in the rain and mud of November, Bapaume was still in German hands, though they had lost over 400,000 men in holding on. The British forces sustained losses of 419,600 including 36,000 Australians, 25,500 Canadians and 10,000 New Zealanders. Amongst the 195,000 French casualties was the American poet Alan Seeger. He had, like so many other Americans, enlisted in the French Foreign Legion to fight in defence of a country he had grown to love. The first, repeated, line of his memorable verse was to come true at Belloy-en-Santerre on 4 July:

> I have a rendezvous with Death
> On some scarred slope of battered hill,
> When Spring comes round again this year
> And the first meadow-flowers appear...

Legionnaire No. 19522 was one of the 869 men of his unit killed in taking the village that day.

While this unimaginable carnage was taking place in Europe, America watched in horror and strove to stay out of the war. 'The man who kept America out of the

The tide of opinion in the USA began to turn against Germany.

Left **New Zealanders inspect a German A7V Sturmpanzerwagen knocked out in front of Amiens where Operation Michael was halted in 1918.**
(TM)

war' was a slogan that helped Woodrow Wilson win re-election as President in 1916. The conflict was already having an impact on the United States. From the beginning there had been a steady flow of American supplies to the British, French, Italians and Russians. When funds to pay for the food, raw materials, arms, ammunition, machine tools and barbed wire ran short, loans were guaranteed by the British Empire. By the spring of 1917 the American economy would have grown by 60 per cent. During the first few months of 1916, German sinkings of merchant ships cost yet more American lives. The President was under pressure to take action, and on 16 April he presented Germany with an ultimatum; unless submarine warfare on commercial vessels ceased, diplomatic relations would be severed. Germany complied. Although still non-combatant, the United States was now inextricably involved.

In the face of the losses sustained by his armies, Falkenhayn withdrew them all along the Western Front early in 1917. Laying waste the land as they went, his

Above **Artillery fire falls on the chalk-marked German trenches on the Somme before the battle commences.** (IWM Q23)

Left **French soldiers, 1915. Left, a private of the 1er Régiment Étranger (Foreign Legion); the Legion later adopted khaki uniform. Right, a private of the 15e Régiment d'Infanterie with corduroy trousers instead of the red worn in 1914, puttees instead of leather gaiters and with the skirts of his greatcoat buttoned back for ease of movement.** (Osprey, MAA 286, *The French Army 1914-1918*) *(Gerry Embleton)*

men fell back to the long, deep complex of trenches and barbed-wire entanglements which became known to their enemies as the Hindenburg Line. This was not a single massive trench system, but a series of prepared positions that linked together from the north-west to the east of France. Each position was protected by fields of barbed wire with alleys which channelled attackers into the firing line of a complex of machine-gun posts. Behind the wire two, three or even four successive lines of trenches were constructed, protected by immensely solid blockhouses and furnished with deep dugouts provided with communicating tunnels and trenches. Facing Arras was the Wotan Position, while running in front of Cambrai and south along the canal to St-Quentin was the Siegfried Position. The

defences continued south of Laon and north of the valley of the Aisne, across the high plateau of Champagne and through the Argonne as the Kriemhild Line. It curved on north of Verdun and then south-east as the Michel Line across the base of the St-Mihiel Salient, protecting Metz. These defences in fact consisted of much more than the lines named here, for there were defensive systems in front of these positions, and yet more behind. It was a formidable series of obstacles behind which Germany could rebuild her strength and launch attacks. Behind this line was the railway which ran from Strasbourg to Metz and, by way of Sedan, to Laon and Cambrai, connecting the German source of supplies to the full length of the front and allowing the swift transfer of troops from one sector to another. Only through Belgium, by way of Liège to Lille and Cambrai, was there an alternative high-volume rail traffic route available to the Germans.

WAR APPROACHES THE NEW WORLD

By the end of 1916 the British blockade of German shipping was cutting deep. The civilian population of the Fatherland was starting to suffer seriously, while American insistence kept the sea lanes to England open for US ships. In Germany, the calculation was made. The United States had no army of significant size and would take years to put forces in the field. An American

declaration of war, if it came at all, was to be risked. Moreover there were plans to extend German threats to North America itself. Even if America entered the war, the task of mobilisation coupled with the fear of invasion would grant Germany the time in which renewed unlimited submarine warfare would inflict crucial damage on Britain and France, and allow her to win before the United States could intervene.

The German Foreign Minister, Dr Alfred von Zimmermann, newly appointed to the post, was very active in January 1917. He was instructing Germany's Ambassador to Mexico to invite the Mexicans to ally themselves with Germany and, by an invasion of the southern United States, regain their former lands of Texas, New Mexico and Arizona. He was also discussing with the German Ambassador in the USA the possibility

Above **British soldiers, 1916. Left, a sergeant of the 1st Battalion, Lancashire Fusiliers with 1908-pattern web equipment, derived from the canvas ammunition pouches introduced by the American, Captain Anson Mills, in the 1880s to replace leather. Right, trench order adopted in cold and muddy winter conditions – goatskin coats and long rubber boots.**
(Osprey, MAA 81, *The British Army 1914-1918*) (Gerry Embleton)

Left **What remained of Delville Wood on 20 September, 1916, after the Battle of the Somme had passed over it.** (IWM Q1156)

Below, left **A French aerial photograph of a German battery and trenches on the Hindenburg Line.** (USAMHI/WWI/28th Div. Griffith, William H.) [10/1]

BATTERIE
ALLEMANDE

of using $50,000 (more than $3,000,000 today) to bribe members of Congress to espouse the German cause. German communication with their Washington Embassy was made by telegraph from the US Embassy in Berlin which sent the message in German cipher to the USA - via London! Meanwhile, messages for Mexico were copied to Washington, using American lines of communication to transmit, in code, what were effectively plans to harm the USA. As it happened, the second of Zimmermann's schemes was frustrated by the delivery of a note by the German Ambassador to US Secretary of State, Robert Lansing, on 31 January declaring that, as from 1 February, unrestricted submarine warfare would be resumed. The first scheme, however, still awaited an outcome.

All through Saturday, 3 February, Walter Page had been waiting for news of his government's reaction to the German note. Darkness fell, blotting out the dreariness of winter, and still no word. Finally, at nine o'clock in the evening, the doorbell rang. The Ambassador's secretary sprang to his feet and rushed downstairs. Admiral William Hall, head of British Naval Intelligence, was hurrying up. 'Thank God!' Hall said as he sped past.

A coded message had come from Washington. Captain Gaunt, the British Naval Attaché there, had sent a cable which Hall read to Page. 'Bernstorff [the German Ambassador] has just been given his passports [i.e. ordered to leave the country]. I shall probably get drunk tonight!' Off the Scilly Isles the American ship *Housatonic* was torpedoed the same day.

British delight was premature. In spite of such clear evidence of hostile German intentions, there was still no declaration of war by the United States. American shipping was reluctant to put to sea and the lucrative trade with the Allies came to a halt. Woodrow Wilson proposed 'armed neutrality', permitting the US Navy and armed merchantmen to fight the U-boats, but nothing more. Clearly he needed encouragement, and Britain provided it.

British Naval Intelligence had broken the German codes. The Zimmermann telegrams had been intercepted as they passed through London (presumably American messages had also been read, though nothing was said about that). On 24 February Ambassador Page telegraphed the President.

Balfour [A.J., later Lord, Balfour, who was now the British Foreign Secretary] has handed me the text of a cipher telegram from Zimmermann... to the German Minister [Ambassador] to Mexico... I give you the English translation as follows: We intend to begin on the first of February unrestricted submarine warfare. We shall endeavour in spite of this to keep the United States of America neutral. In the event of not succeeding, we make Mexico a proposal of an alliance on the following basis: make war together, make peace together, generous financial support and an understanding on our part that Mexico is to reconquer the lost territory in Texas, New Mexico and Arizona...

The telegram went on to instruct the German Ambassador to ask the Mexican President to make approaches to Japan to pave the way for an alliance with Germany. President Wilson released the text of the telegram to the press on 28 February. The effect on the American public was electrifying. Those already in favour of war redoubled their advocacy; those who had hesitated were converted to belligerence. Walter Page added to the pressures on the President on 5 March:

The inquiries which I have made here about the financial conditions disclose an international situation which is most alarming to the financial and industrial outlook of the United States. England has not only to pay her own war bills, but is obliged to finance her allies as well... But she cannot continue her extensive purchases in the United States without shipping gold... and there are... reasons why she cannot make large shipments of gold... Great Britain and France must have a credit in the United States which will be large

enough to prevent the collapse of world trade and the whole financial structure of Europe...

The situation was, in fact, much worse. Britain was close to bankruptcy. Her account with the bankers J.P. Morgan alone was overdrawn by $4 billion, and payment was becoming due. It could not be met.

On 2 April the President addressed Congress. He summarised the unacceptable conduct of Germany, advising that it amounted to waging war against the Government and people of the United States. In the course of his speech he uttered a phrase that brought the house to its feet in enthusiastic applause: 'keeping the world safe for democracy'. Four days later the resolution of Congress for the declaration of war on Germany was signed.

'LAFAYETTE, NOUS VOILA!'

> '**We must go to war in dead earnest. We must sign the Allies' agreement not to make a separate peace, and we must stay in to the end.**'

To declare war was relatively simple. To wage war was an undertaking of immense difficulty. The United States had a regular army of a mere 127,588 men, organised in small units and scattered across the country, with a few small detachments overseas. The National Guard, a reserve similar to Britain's Territorial Force, numbered only 80,436. Furthermore, arming the few men America could put in the field was a problem. There was no heavy artillery at all, few machine-guns, and the issue rifle was the 1903 Springfield. Lee-Enfields, the standard rifles of the British and Empire forces, were already being manufactured in quantity in the USA, but they were of .303-inch calibre whereas the Springfield fired .30 cartridges. It was decided to standardise on the Lee-Enfield; however, this move to a common weapon for British and American forces was immediately devalued by the decision to rechamber the Lee-Enfields to take Springfield cartridges. The sole improvement for the Americans was a move from a five-round to a ten-round magazine. This was only one of a vast number of decisions on supply, transportation, recruitment and organisation that had to be made.

Walter Page had a clear idea of which issues were priorities. He wrote to his friend and former colleague, the publisher Frank N. Doubleday, on 1 April:

Here's the programme:

(1) *Our navy in immediate action in whatever way a conference with the British shows we can best help.*

(2) *A small expeditionary force to France immediately — as large as can be quickly made ready, if only 10,000 men — as proof that we are ready to do some fighting.*

(3) *A large expeditionary force as soon as the men can be organized and equipped. They can be trained into an effective army in France in about one fourth of the time that they could be trained anywhere else.*

(4) *A large loan to the Allies at a low rate of interest.*

(5) *Ships, ships, ships — troop ships, food ships, munition ships, auxiliary ships to the navy, wooden ships, steel ships, little ships, big ships, ships, ships, ships without number or end.*

(6) *A clear-cut expression of the moral issue involved in the war. Every social and political ideal that we stand for is at stake. If we value democracy in the world, this*

is the chance to further it — or bring it into utter disrepute. After Russia [the 'first' Russian Revolution in March had forced the Tsar to abdicate] must come Germany and Austria; and then the King-business will pretty nearly be put out of commission.

(7) *We must go to war in dead earnest. We must sign the Allies' agreement not to make a separate peace, and we must stay in to the end. Then the end will be very greatly hastened.*

This is a very prescient summary of what emerged as American policy, including, unfashionable though it may be today, a statement of the moral basis for putting so many American lives at risk. This moral mission is

also expressed in countless letters and diaries written by men of every rank from private to general, as examination of the archives shows. Reading them is a deeply moving experience.

Not everyone viewed the declaration of war in the same terms. Private Hyman Rosenberg, 28th Infantry Regiment, 1st Division, wrote home to Brooklyn, NY on 17 April 1917 from Panama, where the Americans held the Canal Zone.

Dear Brother Sol,

... I am know a first clas private for the last six months that is $3 a month more and I am a marksman that is $2 a month more and I got a good chance for Corporal or mor than that. Sol, what I think about the war, US will have to get 1,000,000 men befor she can go to fight Germany, and that will take one year at least... Sol you ask me how I like Panama, war is heal Panama is next thing to heal ...

If his spelling was inaccurate, his forecast of the speed of American engagement in the war was remarkably sound, as was his opinion that war is hell.

THE AMERICAN EXPEDITIONARY FORCE

Page's opinion that America had to be seen to move swiftly was shared by the leaders back home. On 28 May the SS *Baltic* sailed from New York with the 191 men who formed the first detachment of the American Expeditionary Force – the Commander-in-Chief and his staff. The operation was meant to be carried out in complete secrecy. Officers were instructed to join in civilian clothes. As a secret it was a failure, not helped

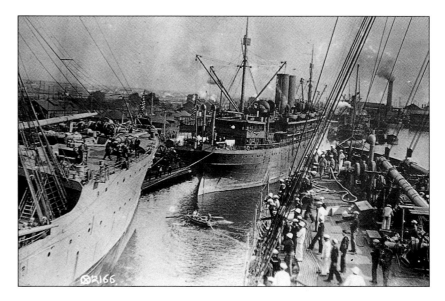

by the fact that quantities of baggage lay about on Pier 60 labelled 'SS *Baltic*, General Pershing's Headquarters'.

Newton B. Baker, Secretary of War, had only two credible candidates from whom to choose for the post of C-in-C, AEF; Major-General Leonard Wood or Major-General John J. Pershing. Wood was, in Baker's view, not only physically unfit but also insubordinate. He had no hesitation in appointing Pershing, for whom physical fitness was almost a fetish. As a tactical officer at West Point in 1897–8 his strictness earned him the nickname of Black Jack. The Commander-in-Chief was 57 years old and had seen service in Mexico and on the

frontier against the Sioux and the Apache, in the Spanish-American War and in the Philippines, as well as in the Russo-Japanese War as an observer. He had further proved his loyalty and obedience in the Punitive Expedition against Mexico of 1916, launched after a raid into New Mexico by Pancho Villa. Tragically, Pershing was a widower, having lost his wife and three daughters in a house fire in San Francisco in 1915 while he had been serving at El Paso; only his son survived.

The raising of a new army had caused the British serious problems which the Americans were determined to avoid. It was immediately decided that reliance on volunteers was not to be risked — men would be drafted into the service. The Draft Bill became law on 18 May, and it was announced that one division would sail as soon as possible. Already the pressure was on for America to supply men to replenish the thinned ranks of her allies, but when Pershing sailed for Europe his orders clearly stated that the AEF was to remain separate and distinct and, as C-in-C, he was specifically charged with the preservation of that status. It was an issue that was to be raised time and again in the coming months.

On the voyage the Americans were kept busy formulating plans and studying the strategic problems they faced. If, as they thought, an army of a million men was to be created, how were they to be supplied? How should Pershing's headquarters be organized, and how should the army itself be structured? Where would they

fight? The post-Civil War US Army had never operated at this level before, so while Pershing and his staff had the opportunity to create a supremely effective military machine, they also faced the daunting challenge of doing so with little relevant experience — a circumstance that is often neglected by critics equipped with hindsight.

The *Baltic* docked at Liverpool on 8 June. After the necessary meetings and introductions in England, Pershing moved on to Paris on 13 June, carrying with him the depressing awareness that the British were either unwilling or unable to give much help toward Page's 'ships, ships, ships'. He arrived to an ecstatic welcome in a country reeling from its most recent setback. On 16 April Joffre's successor as Commander-in-Chief of the French Army, General Robert Nivelle, had launched what was intended to be a knockout blow against the Germans. This had been preceded by a superbly executed and successful Canadian attack on Vimy Ridge on 9 April, and a contemporaneous British attack to the east of Arras which did well at first, but eventually bogged down in snow and mud against the Wotan Position. This distraction failed to ease the problems met by the French. Nivelle's plans for the assault on the Chemin des Dames, north of the valley of the Aisne, were known to the enemy; once the attack was launched the French lost 187,000 men in ten days. The repeated attacks ordered against positions of immense strength sapped French morale, and on 29 April a unit at Châlons-sur-Marne refused orders. The trouble

Above **Hyman Rosenberg, not yet promoted to corporal, wearing American uniform of the pre-war years.** (USAMHI/ WWI/1st Div. 28th Inf. Rosenberg, H.) [8/37]

Left **A pause in the celebratory march through Paris on 4 July 1917. The soldier marked with an X is Private Kyler, and he has captioned the picture 'The Colour Sergeant next to our regimental flag is Sergeant Fink. On his left Private Bailey and Corp. Brozosky, looking to his left.'** (USAMHI/WWI/1st Div. 16th Inf. Coy G. Kyler, Donald D.) [8/30]

Above **The 2nd Battalion, 16th Infantry march through the cheering crowds in Paris.** (USAMHI/ASC 79650) [1/8]

'We all went to the Follies Bergerie, which was quite an experience for me. I had never seen anything like that before.'

spread. The French Army declined to attack any more. Nivelle was sacked and thus it was General Philippe Pétain whom Pershing found in command on his arrival. Pétain acted quickly to quell the mutiny, having some 23,000 soldiers tried by courts martial. Four hundred were sentenced to death and 50 shot, but at the same time Pétain acted to improve the troops' lot, instituting longer periods of rest, more frequent leave and better rations. But for the time being the French Army had become irrelevant as an aggressive force. The burden of continuing the war would fall on the British until France once more, and America for the first time, were ready to share it.

Private Kyler of the 2nd Battalion, 16th Infantry, had landed with the 14,000-strong advance detachment of the AEF at St Nazaire on 26 June. He had enlisted in April, at 16 years of age. They marched to a camp being built by German prisoners two miles from the port, and were housed in buildings with dirt floors and unglazed windows. On 2 July his battalion, together with the regimental band, left by train for Paris, arriving the next day.

We marched at once to a large barrack building which had a courtyard, and a wall around it with a massive iron gate at the entrance. The building had broad hallways and

wide stairs, and was several storeys in height. It had no elevators. I was told that at one time it had housed invalidated French soldiers from Napoleon's army.

The building was Louis XIV's Hôtel des Invalides, one of France's most important military monuments. Further educational experiences were in store. Kyler had no pass, but had little difficulty in slipping out to explore the city. Avoiding a number of invitations to drinks, he eventually became lost.

Then I saw another American soldier whom I knew, with French soldier friends, and I joined them. We all went to the Follies Bergerie, which was quite an experience for me. I had never seen anything like that before.

The next day they were on parade in the Cour d'honneur of Les Invalides, where Pershing, Marshal Joffre, French President Raymond Poincaré and other high officials reviewed them, and flags and gifts were exchanged. A lion cub was the gift of the City of Paris. Kyler did not approve. 'A lion,' he said, 'has no business with an infantry organization at war.'

To the embarrassment of experienced soldiers, the poorly trained troops then set out on a march through Paris. Their lack of precision in drill did not worry the people of Paris. The 'doughboys' – as they were known – were cheered and applauded by thousands of spectators all the way to Picpus Cemetery, burial place of the French general and statesman, the Marquis de Lafayette, who had fought on the Colonists' side in the War of Independence. Pershing spoke little, leaving it to Captain Charles E. Stanton to express America's obligation to the hero of the American Revolution in the words: 'Lafayette, nous voilà!'

Then the soldiers went back to training camp.

Right **The mustachioed Marshal Joffre applauds Major-General John J. Pershing at the tomb of Lafayette, Picpus Cemetery, Paris, 4 July 1917.** (USAMHI/ WWI/1st Div. 16th Inf. Coy G. Kyler, Donald D.) [8/29]

TRAINING AND SUPPLIES

Throughout the next 16 months the military operations of the AEF were to be hampered by two chronic problems: the training of the men, and the provision of the necessary supplies. Each new draft of troops presented a training challenge, while the growing body of men demanded more extensive and sophisticated operations for the supply of arms and ammunition, food, clothing and equipment.

Pershing wrote:

The most important question that confronted us in the preparation of our forces of citizen soldiery for efficient service was training. Except for the Spanish-American War, nearly 20 years before, actual combat experience of the Regular Army had been limited to the independent action of minor commands in the Philippines [mainly against insurgents] and two expeditions into Mexico, each with forces smaller than a modern American division. The World War involved the handling of masses... It was one thing to call one or two million men to the colours, and quite another thing to transform them into an organized, instructed army capable of meeting and holding its own in the battle against the best trained force in Europe with three years of actual war experience to its credit.

Both the French and the British, for obvious reasons of self-interest, were eager to help. Pershing was impressed by the concern of the British to make men proficient in hand-to-hand combat with bayonet and grenade, but felt that British and French alike had too readily accepted trench warfare as the only way in which to conduct the conflict. He therefore tried to

strike a balance between his allies' views and his own concern that training in open warfare should have its proper place.

It was my opinion that the victory could not be won by the costly process of attrition, but that it must be won by driving the enemy out into the open and engaging him in a war of movement...Therefore, we ... undertook to train mainly for open combat, with the objective from the start of vigorously forcing the offensive... My view was that the rifle and bayonet still remained the essential weapons of the infantry...

The effects of these views were to be, on some occasions, grievously costly, and on others magnificently successful. The training of the infantry included not only that of the private soldiers, the 'doughboys', but

Above **Men of the 3rd Battalion, 167th Infantry, 42nd Division, demonstrate their prowess with the bayonet, Villiers-sur-Suze, 4 February 1918.** (USAMHI/ASC 6418) [5/13]

Below **American officers receiving instruction in the use of rifle grenades, British XI Corps School.** (IWM Q222)

Right **Mechanical bakeries (red dots), field bakeries (black), coffee roasting plants (purple) and laundries (yellow) established for the AEF by November 1918.** (USAMHI/Rpt Com. Gen. SOS, May 1919) [8/5.6]

Far right **Rail routes used by the AEF. The blacker the line, the greater its importance and usage. Red dots indicate areas of new construction undertaken by the AEF.** (USAMHI/Rpt Com. Gen. SOS, May 1919) [8/10]

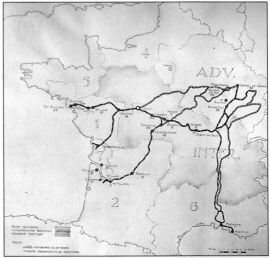

also of their officers, and it was, perhaps, the failure of the latter that led to the loss of so many of the former. Schools were set up for staff and supply as well, for the lack of seasoned officers and experienced staff was a severe handicap. Indeed, it led to the anomaly of US divisions being twice the size of their French or British counterparts, simply because of the shortage of qualified senior staff. The same problem also resulted in US regiments being larger than those of their allies.

Private Kyler, whose opinion on machine-guns has already been given above, was also trained in the use of hand-grenades.

At first it was by French non-commissioned officers, using their grenades, which were of several types. The first *was a training grenade, made of sheet metal... The second type was a fragmentation grenade, made of iron, and with much more explosive power... to be thrown around or behind something, or in a hole or dugout. It would be dangerous to the thrower if it exploded anywhere near him. Another type, heavier and with more explosive power, was for throwing into the openings of caves or fortifications, etc.*

These devices were all pear-shaped, with a pin sticking out of the small end about half an inch. That end had a metal cap covering the pin, secured with sealing wax. When ready to use the grenade, the cap was twisted off and the pin pushed in, which ignited a time fuse. Five to seven seconds after the pin was pushed in the blast would occur. So there was no time to be lost in throwing...

The time available for training was short. Where 12
weeks would have been acceptable, the AEF were lucky
to find nine available once men had landed in France. As
the war went on and demands on American manpower
grew, the training period shortened, perhaps to six
weeks and, in times of crisis, even less.

Private Willard M. Newton of the 105th Engineer
Regiment, 30th Division, from Gibson, North Carolina,
was three weeks short of his 18th birthday and only
two weeks ashore in France when he received instruction in the use of the gas mask.

*June 11... In the afternoon the company is formed and
marched to a gas school... Here we are each issued with a
gas mask. Then we get an hour's instruction and practice in
how and when to use them. To start with an English corporal
or sergeant... takes charge of a platoon and explains the
necessity of the mask, what gas is and how it affects a fellow. Then we are told how to inspect the mask and how to
wear it at the front. After this each platoon is drilled a few
minutes with the mask on. Another short lecture and then
we are thru with this school.*

*On our way back to camp we stop at a supply dump
and get a 'tin bonnet' [steel helmet; US troops used the
British pattern] and 150 rounds of ammunition.*

*June 12. English non-coms [NCOs] instruct in the use of
the rifle in the morning. They explain its make, invention and
how to fire it and numerous other things about it a fellow
should know. Imitation bullets are used in the loading exercise we are given... We leave... at noon...*

And that appears to have been the end of training
with an unfamiliar British Lee-Enfield rifle and an entirely
strange device, the gas mask. Newton does report,
however, a growing familiarity with the French and their
customs. He remarks, 'the French do not drink water at
meal times or any other time.'

Of the 1,981,701 American troops in Europe at the
end of the war, 644,540 were in the Services of Supply
(SOS), which also employed 23,772 civilians. They had
performed a crucial task, too complicated to describe
in detail here, but the scale and challenge of which must
be appreciated. The requirement laid upon Pershing's
willing shoulders to create a discrete and independent
American army meant that, eventually, the AEF would
be responsible for its own section of front line. In the
discussions on the *Baltic* the Lorraine area had been
selected by the American staff as their preferred sector
for action, at least in part because it was accessible. The

Above **The ruins of the ancient Cloth Hall, Ypres in 1918.** (USAMHI/WWI/91st Div. 362nd Inf. Granger, Farley E.) [10/23]

ports of the English Channel were overburdened with the support services for the British on the Somme and in the Ypres Salient, while the north-western ports were clogged with shipping supporting the French war effort. The western coast was relatively uncrowded, as was the south. The systems established by the Americans by the end of the war, as illustrated in the maps in the Report of the Commanding General of the SOS, issued in May 1919, were extensive. They had to fell, extract and distribute the wood needed for construction. They had to build links in a railway system centred on Paris to allow cross-country movement. They had to move armaments and food, fighting men and wounded. They even had to roast coffee.

In the first seven months of the AEF's service in France, shipping was in such short supply that only 484,550 tons of supplies were carried across the Atlantic. By the end of the war the service had improved to the extent that the average for the whole 18 months had risen to 426,000 tons per month. This included 67,825 animals – horses and mules – together with their equipment; 9,500 mule saddles and 335,000 bridles, for example. Automatic weapons and small arms shipped from the USA included 16,393 Browning machine-guns, 6,475 Vickers machine-guns, 19,105 Browning automatic rifles, 278,218 pistols and revolvers and 950,580 rifles. More than 1,000 artillery tractors, ranging from 2.5 to 20 tons, came over, as well as 1,169

The casualties in this, the Third Battle of Ypres, were almost beyond imagination.

trucks of various kinds and more than 300 cars. Then there were a mass of smaller items: hand axes, 425,000; shovels, 1,068,000; cups, 1,005,000; more than 1,300,000 each of knives, forks and spoons. The stores purchased in Europe exceeded, in both weight and number, even those imported from the USA, and all this had to be managed, organised and delivered to keep the army operational.

BLOOD AND MUD AT YPRES

With the exception of limited French attacks at Verdun in August and near the Chemin des Dames in October, the pressure on the Germans on the Western Front for the rest of 1917 was maintained by the British. On 7 June 19 huge mines were exploded under the German defences on the Messines Ridge south of Ypres, and the British, Australian and New Zealand forces thrust the Germans back in what was, with Vimy Ridge, one of the most successful attacks of the war on the Western Front so far. German counter-attacks failed, and the higher land in this flat and featureless country as far as Hill 60, just east of Ypres, thus came into Allied hands once more. In spite of the loss of 24,562 killed or wounded, the British rejoiced. The cost to the Germans was some 23,000 men, of whom 7,264 were made prisoner.

Unhappily, Field Marshal Sir Douglas Haig (as he had by now become) was slow to follow up this success. In part he was restrained by the British Government, wary of public opinion after the fearful carnage of the Somme. In part he wanted to secure his new line before initiating an advance intended to break out into Belgium and neutralise the U-boat base of Zeebrugge. It was not until 17 July that the heavy bombardment of the German lines in front of Ypres started. Over four and a quarter million shells were expended by the time the attack was made on 31 July. And in the week before that it rained, steadily and copiously; the Flanders countryside, with its water table so close to the surface, became a quagmire. In the mud and rain, against furious German counter-shelling and counter-attacks, the advance stalled. The struggle continued through the long summer days and into the autumn. It was not until

November that the original objective, the Passchendaele Ridge, was taken by the Canadians. The casualties in this, the Third Battle of Ypres, were almost beyond imagination. The British, including the Dominion and Empire forces, suffered 244,897 killed, wounded, missing or taken prisoner, the French 8,525. The German Army's strength was reduced by a painful 230,000.

The Allies' situation at that time had become critical. Between 24 October and 9 November the Italians had suffered the massive defeat of Caporetto, losing some 320,000 men (mainly as prisoners), and British reinforcements, as well as French, had to be released to sustain resistance against the Central Powers on the Italian front. The 'second' Revolution in Russia, which happened in November, would clearly take her out of the war; indeed, hostilities on the Eastern Front ceased in the first week of December, which meant that German divisions could now be moved to the Western Front. While these developments took place the AEF had been no more than a token presence in the Allied line. Pressure was now mounting on Pershing to make a reality of the contribution to the war effort that America had pledged to make.

Below **From the Canadian Memorial on Hill 60 the fields and the distant city of Ypres lie quiet in the spring sun.** (MFME Yp/Ar 97 2/9)

Opposite **Sanctuary Wood, where preserved trenches bear witness to war.** (MFME Yp/Ar 97 2/16)

FIRST BLOOD

'At several places along our trench there were narrow tunnels leading downward into the earth to our sleeping places.'

Pershing had not been idle. During August, for example, he had placed an order for 5,000 aircraft with the French Air Ministry, set up an AEF chemical warfare branch and established the General Purchasing Board to centralise buying of supplies for the Army, the Red Cross and the YMCA. By 1 September his headquarters was operational at Chaumont, 150 miles east of Paris, and Pershing moved there five days later. So far the only casualties suffered by the Americans while fighting in the Allied cause were some men hit in an air raid on a British base hospital on 4 September, and two men of the US Engineers caught in shelling while working with the British at Gouzeaucourt on 5 September.

The US 1st Division, then attached to the French 18th Division, at last took its place in the front line on 21 September. The St-Mihiel Salient bulged south-westwards between Verdun and Nancy, and it was at Bathelémont in the Sommerviller sector, north of Lunéville, on 2 November that Donald Kyler of 2nd Battalion, 16th Infantry, had his first experience of the trenches.

The trench system that we entered... had been stable since 1915, and both sides were deeply dug in, with extensive communication trenches, second-line trenches, belts of barbed-wire entanglements, dugouts, and protected gun emplacements... Many of the trees had been broken by shell bursts in the past and the land was pitted with shell holes, partly eroded, and overgrown with weeds.

My platoon was in the company support position. Slightly to our rear was a large dugout where our company command post was located. It was connected by telephone to all our platoon command posts and to the battalion command post. At several places along our trench there were narrow tunnels leading downward into the earth to our sleeping places. To enter, one had to stoop and descend into a dark, damp, smelly hole. When enough depth had been reached the tunnel widened and became level. Short cross tunnels led off of it. There one could sleep if he was tired enough. The whole place was infested with rats, body lice, and bed bugs. At the far end of the tunnel was a shaft and ladder to escape by in case the entrance was caved in by shellfire. Near the entrance to our dugout, and in the opposite direction, a spur trench led to a trench latrine.

On Saturday, 3 November:

I think it was about 3am when suddenly! – the horizon north and east was lit up by a single flash. It was the muzzle blasts of the enemy's guns. No sound was heard for a few moments until the sound wave hit us, and then with a mighty roar it came. The whistling and shrieking of the shells...

Right **The first American soldiers killed in action are buried. A French chaplain reads the service over the bodies of Thomas Enright, Merle D. Hay and James B. Gresham on 20 November 1917.** (USAMHI/ASC 67149) [1/23]

Right **16th Infantry, 1st Division signal rocket gun in the front line, 19 November 1917.** (USAMHI/ASC 67141) [1/19]

The Germans laid a box barrage around the 2nd Battalion's F Company to preclude support from the flanks, and then launched a raid to take prisoners. It was swift, brutal, professional and, unfortunately for the Americans, entirely successful. When the attackers withdrew they took 12 prisoners with them, as well as their own dead and wounded, leaving three Americans soldiers dead and five more wounded. This was their first terrible lesson in trench warfare – the enemy raid to take prisoners for interrogation.

TRENCH WARFARE

The lessons continued. Kyler and a private named Pinaire found themselves assigned to man a listening post the next night. They crawled out through a gap in the wire in front of their trench to a shallow shelter, with orders to observe and listen. They spent five cold nights out there, overhearing enemy patrols, speaking only in whispers and shivering in the damp. Each day, they returned just before dawn and chewed down their supper, which was by then cold and congealed, before making their report. On the third night they were surprised to be approached by a French officer, strolling along without any attempt at concealment. His question, 'Wot would you do in case of fug?' aroused their suspicions and they reported the incident. Next day, while asking questions of other Americans, the supposed officer and his orderly were captured by the

French; identified as German spies, they were duly taken away to be shot.

The combat patrol was the next new experience. About 20 men were chosen, Kyler among them, to mount an ambush on a known enemy patrol route. They blackened their faces and made sure none of their equipment rattled or clanked. Armed mainly with daggers and pistols, they crept out and deployed astride the gully through which the Germans were to come. As the enemy approached, however, someone coughed. The Germans fled under the rattle of American pistol

Right **Gas mask drill for the 16th Infantry, 19 November 1917.** (USAMHI/ASC) [1/22]

Right **An NCO of Sturmbataillon Rohr, May 1916. By order of General Erich von Falkenhayn on 15 May, groups of men from other regiments were seconded for special training in stormtroop tactics, raids and attacks, with this unit. The new steel helmet, the** *Stahlhelm*, **was tested first by the stormtroops in 1915 and the use of puttees and ankle boots, which replaced the traditional jackboot, was also a result of the developments they initiated.** (Osprey, *Warrior 12, German Stormtrooper*) (Gerry Embleton)

fire, and then the ambushers themselves retreated as fast as they could before they became targets. Some became caught in their own wire, and Kyler found himself still outside and tangled in ground wire when:

... an illumination rocket went up from the enemy trench, bathing the area in a bright light. I dived into a nearby shell hole. It was none too soon, because bullets began to hit the rim of that shell hole, and small stones, bits of rusty wire, wooden splinters and dirt showered down on me from the bullet hits above... The fire then ceased. I then had the problem of getting back to our trench without being shot by our men. One does not crawl up to his own trench at night without some sort of announcement: that is — if he wants to live.

Soft whistling and calling his own name did the trick, but even then he found several rifles trained on him when he regained the shelter of his unit's trench.

TANK WARFARE

The only combat arm of a modern army in which the Americans were wholly deficient was armour. When selecting his staff, Pershing had naturally inclined towards men he knew, such as his aide on the Mexican Punitive Expedition, Lieutenant George S. Patton, a man who had been a considerable support to him after the death of his wife and daughters. Captain Patton, as he now was, made a poor staff officer in France and was uncomfortable in the work. He wrote to his wife's cousin:

I have always talked blood and murder and am looked on as an advocate of close-up fighting. I could never look myself in the face if I was a staff officer and comparatively safe.

Right **On the rough grass airstrips accidents were frequent. This aircraft of the US 94th Squadron made a forced landing near Ménil-la-Tour on 3 June, to the delight of French children.** (USAMHI/ASC 17718) [9/9]

Above **American pilots in
training with Curtiss JN-4
'Jenny' aircraft in the USA.**
(USAMHI/ASC 11046/WWI/VI Corps,
Sweeney, Major William R.) [8/17]

The AEF was to benefit from the experience of those 300 of their countrymen who had volunteered to serve France and distinguished themselves in aerial combat.

The decision to establish the US Tank Corps gave him the chance he was looking for to shine in a high-profile post without hanging on to Pershing's coat-tails. He applied to join the corps in October, and few weeks later was sent to Chamlieu to learn from the French. The following January he would set up the AEF Light Tank Center and School at Langres.

As Patton started to get to grips with a new kind of cavalry, the true potential of the tank was being demonstrated by the British at Cambrai. Lieutenant-General the Hon. Sir Julian Byng had three brigades of tanks available to him – 324 battle tanks and over 100 reserves. Nine machines were fitted with radios, although they could only use them when stationary because of the noise the tanks made on the move. There was no preliminary bombardment. On 20 November 1917 a creeping barrage preceded the tanks, while the infantry followed them. The Hindenburg Line was quickly breached, but a low hill in front of the fortified village of Flesquières wrecked the attack. In coming over it, the tanks exposed their lightly armoured undersides to fire from German field guns (there were no specialised anti-tank weapons then). The advance faltered as 28 tanks were hit. The barrage rolled forward relentlessly, leaving the infantry without covering fire and the Germans in control of vital high ground. Territory which had been gained was lost to counter-attacks in the next few days, and the hoped-for breakthrough never came. What had been proved, however, was that tanks had the capability to offer the open warfare for which the Americans yearned.

WAR IN THE AIR

On 3 December Pershing, newly promoted General, arranged to bring the American pilots of the Escadrille Lafayette under US Army command as from the following February. At this time the British and American air forces were still attached to their armies and navies.

Right **An observation balloon
exercise at Camp de Souge
near Bordeaux on 18 April
1918.** (USAMHI/ASC 10276) [9/25]

Americans had been serving in the French Armée de l'Air since the start of the war and in 1916 one of them, Norman Price, an experienced pilot from Massachusetts, along with William Thaw of Pennsylvania, then serving in the French Foreign Legion, and Dr Edmund Gros of the American Ambulance Corps,

masterminded the formation of Escadrille (squadron) N124, which became known as the Escadrille Américaine. Officered by the French, all pilots were volunteers from the, still neutral, United States.

The Germans protested the existence of an American unit when the two countries were not at war, and its name was accordingly changed. Now the AEF was to benefit from the experience of those 300 of their countrymen who had volunteered to serve France and distinguished themselves in aerial combat. Curiously, the majority of the pilots failed American medicals when they joined the AEF and the rules had to be bent in their favour. One pilot was never asked to transfer to the AEF. Eugene Jacques Bullard, the grandson of a slave, was born in Columbus, Georgia. A boxer in Paris when war broke out, he joined the Foreign Legion, winning the Médaille Militaire and the Croix de Guerre at Fort Douaumont before transferring to the aviation service in 1916. In August 1917 he was serving with Groupe de Combat 15, a fully qualified pilot with several victories to his name. The anxiously awaited call for this black American to serve his country never came, however, and it was not until 1992 that he gained recognition from the USA, 31 years after his death.

In 1914, the United States had 23 operational military aircraft, and on the declaration of war a mere 142. The use of French and British aircraft was therefore unavoidable. The American-built DH4 (a British design built under licence) was the only combat aircraft to be

Right **Preparing for
observation: a French officer,
Lieutenant Ludreyt, with an
American, Lieutenant Reed,
equipped with telephone
communication and map
board, ready to ascend.**
(USAMHI/ASC 12277) [9.27]

produced in the USA in significant numbers but, with its central pressurised fuel tank, soon earned the nickname 'Flying Coffin'. More satisfactory was the US-designed and built Liberty engine, a modular design that could be built in any configuration from V-4 to V-12, while its duplicated ignition system meant that it could sustain high levels of damage and continue to operate. As the war progressed the speed of warplane development was staggering. The Germans and the Allies introduced new aircraft to gain advantages of armament, payload, speed, rate of climb, operational ceiling and manoeuvrability. Tactics changed with equal rapidity and by the end of 1916 the lone fighter ace had virtually become a creature of the past. In the early part of that year the British De Havilland DH2 and the French Nieuport XI were supreme, but towards the end of the year a new German concept swung the balance in their favour. Captain Oswald Boelcke introduced the *Jagdstaffel* (a hunting unit, usually abbreviated to 'Jasta'). These large formations of high-performance aircraft were specifically devoted to the destruction of enemy aircraft, particularly the vital but vulnerable two-seaters on reconnaissance or artillery-spotting duties. Boelcke's Jasta 2, using Fokker DIII and Albatros DI biplanes, and including among its pilots one Manfred, Baron von Richthofen, was so successful that Field Marshal Haig warned the War Office in London that new and better aircraft were essential. In 1917 Haig's appeal was met with the introduction of new aircraft for the Royal Flying Corps, the two-seat Bristol F2B and DH4, and the SE5A and Sopwith Camel single-seat 'scouts' (as fighters were called then), as well as new, highly aggressive tactics. These developments were closely observed by Colonel William Mitchell, whom Pershing had tasked with the creation of the AEF aviation programme in June.

MORE MEN, NO ACTION

At the close of 1917, nine months after the USA had gone to war, there were 183,896 men of the AEF in Europe. Since the 1st Division had landed in France in June, the 2nd Division had been formed from 9 and 23 Infantry and 5 and 6 Marine Regiments, and to these had been added the 26th Division in October, the 42nd (Rainbow) Division in November and the 41st, which became 1st Depot Division, on the last day of the year. The French had suffered 569,000 casualties on the Western Front in 1917 and the British 817,790; German losses numbered 883,979. The total of dead, wounded and captured from AEF ranks did not even come to 1,000, while the total of men killed and wounded in action came to 108. It was no wonder that the joy which had greeted the AEF's arrival was changing to doubts about the contribution the Americans intended to make to the overthrow of Germany.

The joy which had greeted the AEF's arrival was changing to doubts about the contribution the Americans intended to make to the overthrow of Germany.

The winter was bitterly cold. Doughboys huddled in inadequate summer clothing while the authorities stateside offered the excuse that winter uniforms were needed for troops in training at home. The steady erosion through casualties of French and British ranks led to renewed argument about the use of the American troops. Pershing gave up to Pétain the four black regiments that were to have formed the 93rd Division, on condition that he could have them back on demand. He never called for them. The British General Sir William Robertson, Chief of the Imperial General Staff (CIGS), proposed to Pershing that, of the 45 divisions being raised in the USA, 15 should be broken up and their troops sent to stiffen British formations. Food shipments could be reduced to free up transportation for them, and by sending only infantry the British need could quickly be met. Pershing proposed instead that the ships be used to bring over full divisions and speed the formation of the American Army, and further asked what number of reserves the British had in England. To have answered truthfully would have been embarrassing, because doubts about Haig's ability to conserve men – indeed, a fear that he willingly squandered them – had led to an unwillingness among senior British politicians to make good the losses of Third Ypres.

The showdown came late in January. Robertson expected an acceptance of the proposal to transport 150,000 infantry for dispersion to British formations. But Pershing stuck to his demand that they be full divisions, that is 90,000 infantry and 60,000 artillery, machine-gunners and other support troops, and that after training with the British they should come under American command. The American adviser to the Allied Supreme War Council, General Tasker H. Bliss, had first supported the British, but now was persuaded that Pershing was right. The British were forced to accept the American plan.

A steady build-up to victory in 1919 was the underlying Allied concept in this winter of 1917–18. The coming months would, however, change everything.

THE GERMAN OFFENSIVE

> ## 'The poor chaps just turned themselves around on their beds and litters gasping, coughing and vomiting...'

Although General Pershing had now obtained the ships to bring more troops, he was still in trouble. The management of the AEF was still close under his own hand, preventing him from devoting himself to making a major contribution to the Allied war effort. As his Chief of Staff, Brigadier-General James G. Harbord said, 'He was getting so busy he had no time for his real job.' In February Pershing thinned down the staff at Chaumont, creating the Service of the Rear (later the Services of Supply) at Tours, allowing his headquarters to concentrate on building the AEF's ability to fight the war. It was not before time.

In January the 1st Division had taken over a realistic sector of the front, eight miles north-west of Nancy at Ansauville on the southern flank of the St-Mihiel Salient. The 42nd Division, with the French in the Champagne region, had their first experience of gas. Dr W. W. van Dolsen, a lieutenant with the 117th Sanitary Train, wrote to his mother on 24 March:

Some of our divisions were pretty badly gassed by mustard gas. It is about the worst there is because although a man may have on his mask it works through his clothing and burns him until his skin is covered with blisters as big as your fist... Ambulances drove up and dropped about 50 gas cases. Some of them had bad shrapnel wounds also and the poor chaps just turned themselves around on their beds and litters gasping, coughing and vomiting; they were as blind as bats (only for the time being) and in great pain... Can you picture giving a man like that an anaesthetic to operate on him?

OPERATION MICHAEL

In 1916 Falkenhayn was sacked as Chief of the German General Staff for his failures at Verdun. He was replaced by Field Marshal Paul von Hindenburg. As a result, General Erich Lundendorff, Hindenburg's First Quartermaster-General and right-hand man, was now effectively the commander of the German forces on the Western Front. He was a man in a hurry. The convoy system for Allied shipping had been introduced in mid-1917, and the losses to U-boats had declined sharply as a result. The British blockade was causing severe shortages in Germany. The Americans were only a token presence as yet, but soon there would be a million

Right **The US 1st Division march to the Ansauville front.**
(USAMHI/ASCO [2/5])

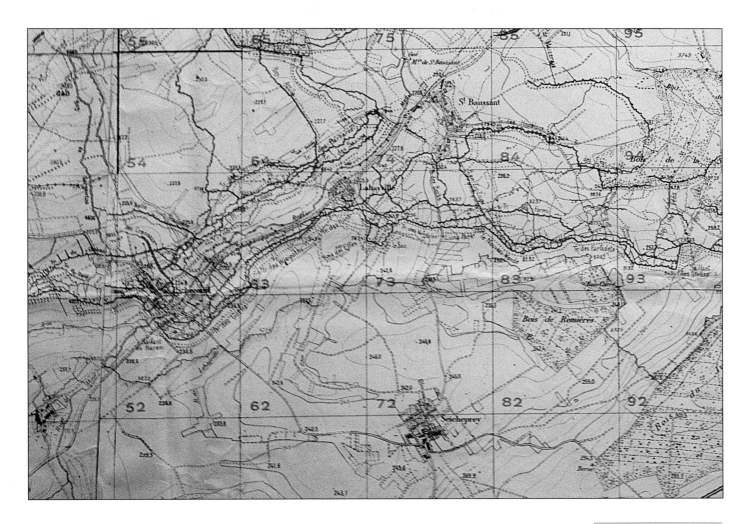

doughboys in France. With the Russians out of the war (the Treaty of Brest-Litovsk, signed on 3 March 1918, completed the Russian surrender), there was time to strike before the French and British were reinforced; there was also the boost of German troops released from the Eastern Front. The control of a continuous railway system from Lille in the north to Strasbourg in the east offered the ability to deliver blows successively in different sectors, moving troops up and down the front as needed. First the British and French were to be divided by hitting the junction between their forces north of Paris, then the former were to be hit again, this time further north, before the French were drawn to the Marne to protect Paris. The final blow was to be in the north once more, throwing the British back to the sea and beyond it, opening the way to a negotiated settlement with the pacifist US President — as he was perceived — Woodrow Wilson. The first of these German blows fell on 21 March.

With no preliminary bombardment to warn them, the 26 British divisions facing the Siegfried Line were hit with the new tactics which had been stunningly successful at Caporetto. Under a rolling barrage, small groups of stormtroops flowed forward, outflanking points of resistance, penetrating the lines and breaking them up in the confusion. Sir Douglas Haig appealed to Pétain for more support in accordance with an unwritten agreement between them, but, justifiably fearful of an attack on Paris, the French Commander-in-Chief declined. The British and French fell back together, doggedly resisting, falling back again, regrouping, and resisting once more. As they did so the 71 German divisions they faced took steady losses. German lines of supply were stretched. Their support troops clambered forward as best they could over a countryside they themselves had laid waste. By 5 April the Germans could do no more and Operation Michael stuttered to a halt. British, Australians, Canadians, and French, with the help of 500 American Engineers, stopped them short of their target, Amiens, key to the Allies' railway system north of Paris.

The reverse they had suffered forced the Allies at last to confront the problem of supreme command. Pershing met Pétain on 25 March and offered him four

Above **Map of the German lines north of Siecheprey (square 71), in blue, and the American front line, in red, as at 20 March 1918. Detail of the Aliies' trenches was omitted for security reasons. The Bois de Remières is shown in square 82.**
(USAMHI/MFME MF1/8)

divisions to help meet the crisis of Operation Michael. But Pershing was not present the following day when Pétain, General Ferdinand Foch, Poincaré and Georges Clemenceau (respectively France's President and Prime Minister) met the British, Haig, General Sir Henry Wilson (who had succeeded Robertson as CIGS in February) and Lord Milner, a member of the British War Cabinet, at Doullens. It was there agreed that Foch should become co-ordinator of the military operations, a responsibility that was increased to the strategic direction of the Allies in April. Pershing, while excluded from the making of the decision, doubtless welcomed its logic, but he was not in the least happy with what emerged from the talks that subsequently took place between Bliss and General Sir Henry Rawlinson (at that time the British military representative on the Supreme War Council). The outcome of that meeting was an agreement that America would send only infantry and machine-gun units to France until further notice. The prospects for creating an American Army in France were seriously damaged, but Pershing, in the face of the current crisis, had to agree, and made an emotional declaration of support to Foch.

Almost as soon as the attempt on Amiens had failed, the Germans launched Operation Georgette. They had intended a more substantial effort in the north on the River Lys, but the casualties of Operation Michael forced them to scale down their attack. Nonetheless it came perilously close to success at the outset. On 9 April 14 German divisions struck between Armentières and Béthune. The line broke at Laventie, 11 miles west of Lille, where a Portuguese unit gave

way, and the action developed north-west to Estaires as the British 55th Division stood firm to the south. Haig was determined that the attempt to break through to the Channel would fail. On 11 April he issued his famous Special Order '...to fight it out! Every position must be held to the last man: there must be no retirement. With our backs to the wall, and believing in the justice of our cause, each one of us must fight on to the end.' By the end of the month most of the territory around Ypres so bloodily gained the previous year had been lost, but the Germans had failed to break through and had lost another 109,300 men in addition to the 239,000 casualties of Operation Michael. Men they could hardly spare.

On the St-Mihiel front the US 1st Division was relieved by the 26th in an operation noted for its confusion, emphasising how much was still to be learnt by the AEF. The Yankee Division was in place on 3 April and, in its turn, was introduced to trench warfare. Various raids and counter-raids gave the 26th good reason to be proud of their abilities, but on 20 April they were given a terrible lesson. A huge bombardment, which began at about 3am, preceded an attack by German troops not merely raiding, but intending to take and hold the American lines at Siecheprey. Nearly 3,000 assault troops hit the two companies of doughboys and ripped them apart, taking the little town. To the north-east the Germans had failed to throw the Americans out of the Bois de Remières and the men of the 104th Infantry Regiment fought back, hand-to-hand, and regained their former front line. The counter-attack planned for the morning of that day, 21 April, was abandoned by a major who was too confused to carry it out, but the Germans, having lost the wood, were now in a difficult position, and therefore chose to withdraw. When the 26th regained their trenches and counted the cost, their losses came to 81 killed, 187 wounded, 214 gassed and 187 missing. The action fuelled the doubt in their allies' minds about the abilities of the AEF.

CANTIGNY

The United States had now been at war for a year. In that time the AEF's fatal casualties in action had been a mere 163 men. It was essential that Pershing take a greater share of the load. It was even more important that he gain the confidence of his allies and raise the morale of his troops by making a successful attack. The fighting spirit of the men was not in doubt, but the competence of the regimental officers and staff was. The place chosen for this first American offensive was the village of Cantigny, west of Montdidier, where the German advance had been halted in March. The 1st Division had entered the line here on 23 April, overlooked by the Germans from the village on the ridge.

'Several men were killed, one was gone completely... he was in right where the shell hit...'

Raymond Austin of the 6th Field Artillery wrote to his mother in May:

The German drive advanced so rapidly that the people ... left in great haste. Their houses and their household goods were abandoned – china, bed linen, clocks, furniture, pianos and everything... My dugout is very novel – a wine cellar cut from pure, white chalk...

This section of the front was, in terms of this war, quiet. Austin's battery was firing some 1,500 rounds a day and the Germans were no less energetic. Earl D. Seaton, 16th Infantry, was checking the food issue in Broyes when shells started to fall.

At first at the edge of the town, then closer and closer the shells landed... We heard the 'whomp', then the topoff as the shell reached its highest and started down, growing louder and louder. Then the sharp crack as it hit the tile roof and exploded before entering the ground... Several men were killed, one was gone completely... he was in right where the shell hit... I saw a leg with shoe and puttee leggings on it, cut off above the knee. One fellow told me he was walking down the street with his mess kit when the fellow in front of him was cut off at the hips. The legs stood for a moment, as the blood oozed out, then collapsed.

Captain Jeremiah M. Evarts, 18th Infantry, was concerned about one of his men, Private Jackson. Every time the shelling started up the boy shook uncontrollably. He threw himself flat in the bottom of the trench and when Evarts pulled him up the tears were flowing.

That night I made him go the rounds with [Sergeant] Shea and myself. I walked first and Shea last. Poor Jackson was frightened most of the time and if a shell came within 200 yards, he was flat on the ground. It was still raining and Shea was greatly annoyed after he had fallen over Jackson several times in the dark.

The French provided the greater part of the artillery support for the coming attack. The preparations were made with immense care – the American staff, including Captain George C. Marshall, Jr, were determined that everything should go perfectly. A model of the objective was made for the officers and NCOs to study and, well to the rear, the target zone was replicated by tracing it out on the ground so that troops could practise their tasks. The mission was described and repeatedly emphasised – Cantigny was to be taken and held against all counter-attacks. The assault on 28 May fell to the 28th Infantry Regiment.

Below **The village of Cantigny from the American front line, 15 May 1918.** (USAMHI/ASC 14210/WWI/1st Div. 16th Inf. Seaton, Earl D.) [8/33]

Raymond Austin wrote home on 1 June:

We adjusted our rolling barrage, etc., as discreetly as possible the day before, and everything was ready that evening... H hour would be at 6.45am – the time when the infantry would go over the top... At 4.45 all batteries... began their final adjustments all along the line and at the first shots the Boche's sausages [observation balloons] went up in a hurry to see what was going on... Then at 5.45 all batteries began a heavy raking fire throughout the zone to be covered by our advance. The ground was pounded to dust by our shells... At 6.40 the preparation ceased, the heavy batteries shifted over to cover the flanks of the attack or pounded the enemy rear trenches and batteries, and the 75s [shells from French 75-mm field guns, the famous 'Soixante-Quinzes'] dropped into place on the line of departure of the rolling barrage... until along the whole front of the attack there was a perfect, even line of bursting shells a mile long. Then at 6.45... the barrage moved forward at a rate just fast enough for the infantry to keep up with it at a walk. At the same time... the infantry suddenly appeared on the slope of the ridge close behind our barrage – a long brown line with bay-onets glistening in the sun... They walked steadily along... accompanied by the tanks which buzzed along with smoke coming out from their exhausts and their guns. As the line reached the crest and was silhouetted in the morning sun... it looked like a long picket fence. Occasionally a shell would strike among them and a gap would appear among the pickets, then quickly close.

The Americans were soon in the enemy's third-line trenches, having carried the first and second lines. As the shellfire passed beyond Cantigny, Germans emerged from the cellars where they had sheltered, either of their own volition or flushed out by flamethrower or grenade, and a flurry of fights saw them either killed or captured. Now the 28th had to hold the ground. Counter-attacks were not long in coming, the German shelling was immediate. Lieutenant Daniel Sargent, 5th Field Artillery, saw the clouds of yellow smoke rising from the ruins of the town. As the shells began to fall nearer to him and his companions, a French officer and another American lieutenant, the latter asked him the date of his commission. 'September, 1917,' Sargent replied.

'But,' came the reply, 'my commission was dated August, 1917, which makes me your senior, in which case I suppose this foxhole falls to me.'

With that the speaker occupied the only available cover. The Frenchman witnessed this exchange with total incredulity before departing. The French artillery had been called away, because only a few hours before, the Germans had launched their next great assault, Operation Blücher-Yorck, this time on the Chemin des Dames above the valley of the Aisne. Every French gun was needed to oppose the latest German assault.

There were two counter-attacks that day and the 28th fought both of them off. Two companies of the 18th Infantry reinforced the position that night, and Captain Evarts took his men forward as part of a fur-ther reinforcement the night after. Jackson shook, did not cry, and managed to stay with his buddies. Evarts

Below **Château-Thierry and the valley of the Marne from the American Memorial on Hill 204. The river curves to the left, crossed by the rebuilt bridge to the island on the right from which another bridge takes the road southwards.** (MFME Yp/Ar 6/36)

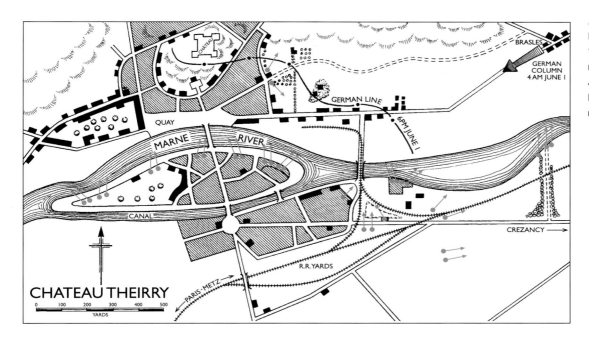

Left **Château-Thierry, 1 June 1918. From J. R. Mendenhall's map in** Infantry Journal, **Jan./Feb. 1936, p. 17. Machine-gun positions marked in red.**

was proud of him. In all there were seven attempts by the Germans to regain the ground. All failed. Some 50 casualties had been the price of taking Cantigny, but holding it cost the Americans 199 killed, 652 wounded, 200 gassed and 16 missing. Raymond Austin wrote:

Casualty lists of an attack like this don't look very large beside those of a German 50-mile-front drive, but when you see fine, young American boys lying dead in heaps of six or eight or twelve here and there it's more than enough, but it must be if we're going to whip Germany and the sooner people realize it in America the better – and we may be able to finish the job sooner.

It was, as Austin points out, a minor action, but it made its point. The Americans had proved not only that they could organise and carry out an attack, but also that they could hold their ground.

HOLDING THE LINE – OPERATION BLÜCHER-YORCK

In peacetime, the direct route from Soissons to Reims runs along a high ridge, the Chemin des Dames. To the south the land falls away steeply to the Aisne, which had been soaked with the French blood of Nivelle's ill-judged attack in 1917. It had now become a quiet front, held by four divisions of the French Sixth Army and four British divisions of IX Corps, all of them 'resting'. Reconnaissance was neglected; no aerial photographs had been taken for two months and even ordinary observation flights had not been made for a month. General Ludendorff gathered 30 divisions for the attack, planned as the penultimate thrust before destroying the British in Flanders. At 1am on 27 May the shells crashed down and the Germans swept forward. Their success

was terrifying. By noon they were on the Aisne and by dark on the Vesle. On 28 May they were over that river and heading for the Marne, which they reached two days later. It was a rout, although in places resistance was heroic. At Ville-aux-Bois-les-Pontaverts two British units, the 2nd Battalion, the Devonshire Regiment and 5th (Gibraltar) Battery, 45 Brigade, Royal Field Artillery fought to the last man either killed or captured. Both units were honoured with the Croix de Guerre. The Kaiser himself visited the viewpoint of the California Position, high above the village of Craonne, to relish the victory of his army. The German flood now looked as if it would reach as far as Paris.

The Allied Supreme War Council met in Versailles on 1 June and General Bliss asked Pershing to attend. The discussions were heated and incoherent. Foch demanded that the Americans rush even untrained troops to France; Pershing insisted on the maintenance of a balanced force, bringing over men for the Services of Supply as well as front-line troops, and declared himself willing to fall back to the River Loire if necessary. It is now clear that if this balanced growth had not been agreed, the American Army would not have been able to function later that year. In the meantime two AEF divisions, the 2nd and 3rd, were heading at speed for the Marne.

Just after noon on 31 May, the 7th Machine-Gun Battalion of the 3rd Division was at Condé-en-Brie, having come 110 miles north in 22 hours in their Model T Ford trucks. Château-Thierry, where bridges crossed the Marne, lay eight miles east. A stream of refugees and broken troops was heading south. The Americans pushed on, but the gravity fuel feed of their trucks let

The German flood now looked as if it would reach as far as Paris.

As dusk fell the fighting had become a hand-to-hand struggle on the bridge itself.

them down when, with nearly empty tanks, they encountered a steep hill. They unloaded their weapons and ammunition and went forward on foot. At Nesles-la-Montagne, overlooking the open flood plain of the Marne, they found a French battery engaging German positions north of the river. South of the main stream of the Marne, an island is formed by a canalized branch of the river. Captain Charles H. Houghton made his way forward over the bridge on to the island. From there he moved to the main bridge over the Marne, facing the market square of Château-Thierry, tucked under the hill on which stands the castle that gives the town its name. North of the town other hills rose steeply. A second bridge, carrying the railway, spanned the river east of the island. Houghton made contact with the French 52nd Colonial Division whose commander, General Marchand, ordered him to deploy on the north bank of the island and south of the east bridge to cover the retreat. The bridges were being prepared for demolition by French forces. By 4.30pm on that day, the first elements of 7th Machine-Gun Battalion were in place, and one section of A Company (commanded by Lieutenant John T. Bissell), together with a French unit, was north of the east bridge to cover the north-eastern approaches to the town.

At about 4am on 1 June the Germans marched confidently forward in a column along the road from Brasles, on the northern bank of the Marne, to enter Château-Thierry. The machine-guns opened fire, slicing great gaps in their ranks, and they flung themselves into the wheat crop at the side of the road. During the long day, a series of attempts to take the northern end of the east bridge developed. Shellfire fell on the American positions south of the river. The Germans slowly pushed the French back through the town, past barricades of furniture built across the streets, until a small enclave around the northern end of the west bridge remained. As dusk fell the fighting had become a hand-to-hand struggle on the bridge itself, when, with a great roar, the bridge was blown up. The American machine-guns swept the square on the opposite bank where the Germans were milling around in great numbers. Lieutenant Bissell and his men were approaching the west bridge on the enemy's side of the river as it blew; the Germans saw them and a cat-and-mouse pursuit through the shattered streets took place before Bissell brought his men back over the east bridge. During the brief pause in machine-gun fire which was necessary to let them cross, a party of Germans were able to follow. Lieutenant John R. Mendenhall, commanding B Company, had his work cut out to reorganise the defence, for a gap had opened between American units deployed south of the river. Fortunately the Germans were not aware of the opportunity, and the regrouped machine-gunners drove them back. The battle continued throughout the next day, and at times the Hotchkiss guns of B Company glowed cherry red, so heavy was their fire. In the evening of 3 June charges placed on the abutments of the east bridge by the French that day were fired. The passage of the Marne was barred to the enemy.

On 7 May, Brigadier-General Harbord achieved his ambition to get a field command, leaving his post as Chief of Staff to Pershing and taking command of 4 Marine Brigade, 2nd Division. Now, 31 May, he found himself, with others of Major-General Omar Bundy's 2nd Division, hurrying from their intended relief of the 1st at Cantigny toward the advancing Germans northeast of Paris. The road from Château-Thierry to Paris, the N3, climbs the steep hill westwards, leaving Hill 204 (on which the American monument now stands) to the left, passes through the village of Vaux and away between Coupru to the south and Lucy-le-Bocage to the north. Parallel to it some three miles north, the little River Clignon runs through a narrow valley, passing through Torcy-en-Valois and Bussiares, affording a sheltered route west for forces driving from the east. On 1 June General Jean Degoutte, commanding the French XXI Corps, charged his 43rd Division with the defence of the line from the north-west to the south-east,

Above **A Company, 7th Machine-Gun Battalion, 3rd Division, in position on the island at Château-Thierry with a Hotchkiss machine-gun, 1 June 1918.** (National Archives/ASC 14118)

Right **Captain Hyatt, F Battery, 15th Field Artillery, 2nd Division, with a megaphone, and a signaller at Coupru, 5 June 1918.** USAMHI/ASC 14191) [4/8]

astride the valley through the villages of St-Gendeloulph, Bussiares, Torcy, Belleau and Bourresches. They could not hold it. He was given the 2nd American Division to solve the problem and ordered them to hold south of the Bois de Belleau – Belleau Wood – and to block the main road. Harbord's Marines made for Lucy-le-Bocage on the Belleau side, and the US 3 Infantry Brigade took on the southern sector, with the French 167th Division on the 2nd Division's left.

Private William A. Francis, a 20-year-old born in Dallas, Texas, was a sharpshooter with the 5th Marines. He recalled their confusing arrival.

We left the trucks and hiked through the woods to keep out of sight of the German airplanes... It was about dusk and we were ordered to throw our packs away, keeping our blankets and emergency rations... It is now dark; a company of Marines has just passed, everyone silent, for we realize that most of us will never return... We are marching in single file, *it is very dark and we have to march with one hand on the shoulder of the man in front of us to keep from getting lost... The [field telephone] line has been broken several times; runners have gone out to find the other part of the line... It has settled down to a slow, steady rain, and we are soaking wet. We finally reached a little town named Lucy...*

The Marines hastened to get organised. Seeking advice from a French officer, a Marine was startled to receive counsel to retreat. 'Retreat, hell! We just got here,' was the response. Just who gave that answer is not clear. Perhaps it was Colonel Wendell C. Neville, or maybe Captain Lloyd S. Williams. Private Malcolm C. Aitken of the 5th Marines attributed it to Lieutenant-Colonel Frederick Wise. Whoever said it captured the American attitude in a nutshell.

For the next three days and nights the Marines consolidated their positions and beat off repeated German attacks. William Francis tells of three nights of raids:

The Germans came down the hill firing everthing at us, machine-guns, rifle and hand grenades. We opened up immediately with our rifles and threw hand grenades as if they had been baseballs. We could not see them, but we knew they were only a few yards away and they were set upon taking our trench... This lasted all thru the night ... We were nearly exhausted for sleep, none of us having slept for days... It was impossible to get chow to us, so we had to eat whatever we could find, one of the boys found a piece of fat bacon covered with dirt and filth; we cleaned it off and fired it over canned heat, and believe me it surely tasted good.

On 5 June, Harbord was ordered to take Belleau Wood. French sources declared it to be lightly held and to have little artillery support. It was thus thought to be vulnerable to a surprise attack. In actual fact it was occupied by the whole German 461st Regiment, more than 1,000 men. On the morning of 6 June the Marines moved forward and established a position facing the wood across a wheatfield. Private Malcolm D. Aitken, of San Jose, California, crossed that field.

The enemy could not be seen except occasionally, but their presence was sorely felt. Several faces were here but Duke and Jim as well as my bunckie [buddy] had mysteriously

'You could hear them (our men) calling for help for hours, and finally each call became faint and finally stopped...'

disappeared. I saw my first death, and it was a shock. There were so many more that suddenly dropped and were gone within the minute, however, that I did not notice it anymore. They were dropping all around me... How the handfull ever reached the hill top I never knew, but there we were... On

Right **Comrades in arms. On the left, Arthur Murphy and, on the right, Private Malcolm C. Aitken of the 5th Marines. Both survived the war, but Murphy was killed in an accident soon after returning home.** (USAMHI/WWI/2nd Div. 5th Marines, Aitken, Malcolm C.) [8/ 12]

Far right **A US 2nd Division marker in Belleau Wood.** (MFME Yp/Ar 7/7)

Below **The memorial to the US Marines in Belleau Wood – officially renamed Bois de la Brigade de Marine in their honour.** (MFME Yp/Ar 7/16)

roll call the middle of the morning [next day] there were 20 of the 250 that started here.

The Marines had taken the edge of the wood and the village of Bourreches at the south-eastern corner, at a cost of 1,087 men killed, wounded or captured. Just to the south the 23rd Infantry, misunderstanding their orders to maintain contact with the Marines' flank, had pushed too far forward in their enthusiasm and had been badly mauled, losing 27 killed and 225 wounded or missing. On 8 June the Marines tried again, but gained no ground.

The attacks of the following days were preceded by artillery bombardments that shattered the trees and struck sparks off the rocks, but did little to shake the Germans. Units repeatedly lost orientation in the confusion of smashed woodland. William Francis describes the fighting.

We crawled on all fours, Indian fashion, and kept going without seeing the enemy. Everything was as still as death. We had crawled a good piece this way when all of a sudden it sounded as though all hell had broken loose – all the machine-guns the enemy had opened up on us... They knew as soon as we had left our trench and had waited until we had gotten far enough out... I saw a little rock in front of me that would afford a little protection so I made for this... I was trying to work close enough to use my bombs [grenades], for a rifle was useless on account of the brush being too thick... I looked around to see if I could locate some of our men, and about this time a boy crawled up to me – we were the only two left of our squad... About five hundred feet from here was a big rock, we slipped around this to see if our men were there – or Germans and to our great relief we found eight of our men. It was now dark and we had no idea where we were so we decided the only thing to do was to stay and defend ourselves as best we could...We could hear men in 'No Man's Land' calling for help. It was impossible to go for them for we had no idea where the Germans were...You could hear them (our men) calling for help for hours, and finally each call became faint and finally stopped – they had died.

The Germans were as determined as the Americans to win at Belleau Wood. They regarded it as vital to show both their enemies and their own comrades that the much-feared Americans could be beaten. But after two weeks of gruelling combat both sides were exhausted. As the Germans relieved their severely battered troops the Marines were also granted a brief respite, being relieved by the 7th Infantry from 3rd Division. It gave them a chance to bury the dead. Malcolm Aitken was on a burial detail.

We buried skads of them this morning [15 June], some very badly decomposed as they had been in the hot sun for two days. They were bluish-black in color and the odor beggars description...After laying them side by side 40 or so to a 6ft trench we stood with uncovered heads while the service, short and to the point, was recited... Just as the final prayer was being recited the first of a bracket of three shells lit a little in front... the third of the group made a direct hit on our beautiful trench. Two of the detail were killed and three wounded. We buried the pieces and said some more hurried prayers, took our wounded to the PC [Post of Command], reported the casualties and here we are. C'est le Guerre.

When the Marines moved back into the line on 22, 23 and 24 June no great change in position had been achieved. Renewed attacks simply confirmed the strength of the German positions.

At long last the desire to take the wood was to be supported with the means to do so. The 2nd Division now had three French batteries – two of the 37th Light Artillery and one of the 333rd Heavy Artillery – and for 14 hours from 3am on 25 June they pounded the German lines in the northern half of Belleau Wood. At 5pm the attack went in behind a rolling barrage. William Francis was there:

About 700 of us went over this time – all that was left of our battalion... We had orders to take no prisoners... We had a wonderful barrage from our artillery which was falling only a few yards in front of us...We finally made it to the top of the hill; the Germans were entrenched at the bottom of the hill and just beyond the hill was a large wheatfield, the wheat being about waist high. After we had reached the top of the hill the Germans opened up with their machine-guns, hand and rifle grenades and trench mortars. Just then we all seemed to go crazy for we gave a yell like a bunch of wild indians and started down the hill running and cursing in the face of the machine-gun fire. Men were falling on every side, but we kept going, yelling and firing as we went. How any of us got through ... I will never be able to figure out... I found a bunch of Germans in their dugout and ran them out... How we did cut the Germans down when they tried to cross the wheatfield. The wheat was just high enough to make good shooting, and when we hit one he would jump in the

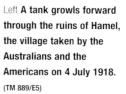

Left **A tank growls forward through the ruins of Hamel, the village taken by the Australians and the Americans on 4 July 1918.**
(TM 889/E5)

Right **Many aircraft accidents
were trivial, the light
machines suffering little
damage even when flipped
upside down in a rough
landing. Here, at Toul, men of
the 94th Squadron turn an
aircraft the right way up.**
(USAMHI/ASC 11315) [9/0]

Right **Many aircraft accidents
were trivial, the light
machines suffering little
damage even when flipped
upside down in a rough
landing. Here, at Toul, men of
the 94th Squadron turn an
aircraft the right way up.**
(USAMHI/ASC 11315) [9/0]

air like a rabbit and fall. We had orders to take no prisoners, to kill all of them, but it was impossible for we had no idea there were so many Germans there.

That the Americans had the guts and the skill to fight was now beyond doubt, but it had cost 4 Marine Brigade half its strength to prove it. For Ambassador Page in London the victory was tarnished by grief. His nephew, Sergeant Alison Page, serving with the Marines, was killed in the taking of Belleau Wood.

VAUX AND HAMEL

The capture of Vaux on 1 July was a very different business. There had been a month to become familiar with the territory and to regroup after the scramble to block the German advance. There was time to make precise plans. The displaced citizens of the village were quizzed to reveal the precise layout of every street and house in the place. The artillery was in place and communications were well organised. The 23rd Infantry was on the left, from Bourreches to the Triangle brickyard north of what is now the N3, the 9th was on the right with the 2nd Engineers in support, and the French beyond them with Hill 204 as their objective. A 13-hour artillery barrage started at 5am. This converted to a rolling barrage when the attack went in and a standing barrage beyond the village to prevent counter-attacks once it had been taken. Vaux was in American hands in an hour.

Private Ralph L. Williams was with the 2nd Engineers. Just before they moved forward

...A newsreel photographer worked his way along the ravine bottom, stopped in front of us and said that this looked like a good place. He asked if he could get past us and I asked him where he was going. He said, 'Over the rim. I'm

going to take movies of the attack.' We gave him a hand and right in the thick of the firing, the chap crawled over and we handed the rest of his gear to him. What guts that fellow had!

The attack went in at 6pm. The first thing Williams saw was the scattered equipment and dismembered body of the photographer where a shell had made a direct hit.

My squad had demolition equipment: dynamite, triton, caps, drills and a magneto with which to blow up buildings. We found out later Joe was carrying the dynamite, which weighed about 25 pounds, and was right beside me. I was carrying a sack of percussion caps, more dangerous than the dynamite, and the magneto. None of us knew what we were carrying at the time. Joe was knocked down twice when shells landed in back of him, and he fell again crawling over some German wire. Luck was with us all, and our squad made it...

They had orders to blow up the German head-quarters building if the occupants did not surrender, but surrender they did when an irate Irishman who had lost his best buddy started lobbing grenades through the windows. Williams was ordered to take the prisoners to the rear, and when he returned was deeply disappointed to have missed the souvenir hunt. There were:

...lugers, spiked helmets, and dress uniforms with long flowing capes. It seemed every soldier had gotten some souvenir out of it – except me!

The French 153rd Infantry Regiment had a harder time against the heights of Hill 204 and were forced to dig in without clearing the hill. When the US 2nd Division was relieved on 4 July a small gas balloon floated over from the German lines and landed; attached to it was the message, 'Goodbye, Second – Hello, Twenty-sixth.' Their information was correct.

'I believe it is the first time American troops fought side by side with their enemy of our own revolutionary days, the British.'

Above **An American military aviator of VII Corps Aero Service, 1918. Aviators were in the Signal Corps and wore that insignia on the collar, and, after 27 October 1917, two silver wings with a shield and star on the breast. The wings and propeller collar badge was introduced in June 1918. The chevrons denote a year of overseas service.** (Osprey, *MAA 230 US Army 1890-1920*) *(Jeffrey Burn)*

That day was important not only far to the west on the Somme front, but also in the conduct of the war itself. The British front line east of Amiens needed to be straightened out before a major attack could be contemplated. This was because the salient at the village of Hamel offered the Germans the opportunity to enfilade an advance from the west. The mission was given to the Australian Army Corps under Lieutenant-General Sir John Monash, a man whom Haig, among others, admired for his meticulous staff work and the aggressive creativity of his plans.

Monash held that the infantry should be given the task of holding ground, protected in their advance by the best that technology could provide and unhampered by needlessly heavy loads. The attack was to go forward, after minimal softening up by artillery, behind a creeping barrage, which tanks were to follow with infantry in support. The 4th Australian Division provided the infantry, 60 British Mark V heavy tanks were deployed and the machine-gun battalions of the 2nd, 3rd and 5th Australian Divisions were added to deal with counter-attacks. The plans were detailed and precise, but were endangered at the eleventh hour. The American 33rd Division had been training with the Australians and two companies from the 131st and two from the 132nd Infantry were included in the operation. Pershing wrote, '... the British made constant efforts to get [our troops] into their lines.' He did his best to prevent their involvement in Monash's attack, but plans were too far advanced to permit their withdrawal. For their part, the men of the 33rd, of course, were determined not to be left out!

The attack at Hamel on 4 July was a minor masterpiece. The barrage was perfectly planned and controlled, the tanks performed exactly as intended and the infantry mopped up the surviving German defenders. A Congressional Medal of Honor (America's highest award for gallantry) was won at Hamel that day. Corporal Thomas A. Pope charged a stubborn machine-gun nest, killed half the crew with the bayonet and held the rest at gunpoint until his section came up to make them prisoner. The Australian machine guns were supplied with a further 100,000 rounds of ammunition by the Royal Air Force (newly created on 1 April by amalgamating the Royal Flying Corps with the Royal Naval Air Service) in the first such air-drop in history. The whole operation took 93 minutes. Monash is said to have been irritated by the additional, unplanned, three minutes. The taking of Hamel was a model of combined artillery, tank, infantry and air operations. Pershing grudgingly admitted that the behaviour of the American troops was splendid, but made no comment on the skill of Monash.

Will Judy of Chicago was serving as a clerk with the staff of the 33rd Division. He wrote:

Companies A and G of the 132nd Infantry marched into our headquarters this morning, dirty, tired and wild-eyed... The men were quiet; they seemed in melancholy; the glory of battle was not on their faces. Every one carried a souvenir – a cap, a button, a badge, a gun captured from the enemy... The battle has historical importance for I believe it is the first time American troops fought side by side with their enemy of our own revolutionary days, the British.

OPERATION FRIEDENSTURM – PEACE STORM

The unexpected success of Operation Blücher-Yorck in early June, though now halted, encouraged Ludendorff to attempt a new thrust to cross the Marne and threaten Paris. The effort made on 9–14 June north of Paris, known as the Battle of the Matz or Operation Gneisenau, between Noyon and Mondidier, had been thrown back by a brilliant flanking attack devised by the French General Charles Mangin, using a force of 163 tanks and air support with his four divisions. The northerly route to Paris was thus closed. The fifth major German offensive of the year, Friedensturm, was directed east and west of Reims. Allied intelligence was good; the offensive was expected.

The attack, on 15 July, on the Champagne front to the east of Reims, failed entirely. General Henri Gouraud had adopted Pétain's concept of the recoiling buffer; defence in depth with the front line lightly held and progressively stronger positions to the rear. German shelling fell on largely empty trenches and the advance ran into pockets of defenders which sapped the German infantry's strength as they struggled forward through the shell-pocked forward line. The French Fourth Army, with the American 42nd Division under command, halted them.

East of Château-Thierry, the southern bank of the Marne was held by General Degoutte's French Sixth

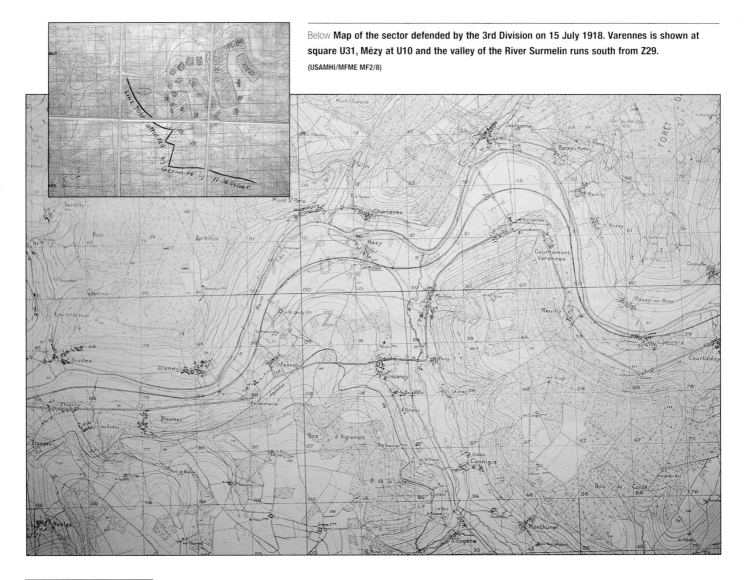

Below **Map of the sector defended by the 3rd Division on 15 July 1918. Varennes is shown at square U31, Mézy at U10 and the valley of the River Surmelin runs south from Z29.** (USAMHI/MFME MF2/8)

Insert, above **German objectives for 15 July 1918, from a map captured by the 3rd Division and annotated by them. The red hash shows areas to be bombarded by trench mortars and 'fog' and the blue areas to be shelled with gas.** (USAMHI/MFME 7/25)

Army. It was stiffened with elements of the American 28th Division and Major-General Joseph T. Dickman's 3rd Division in the sector from Château-Thierry to Varennes, at the top of the great northerly curve in the river. On Dickman's right were the French, in whom he reposed small confidence. Next to the French he placed his 38th Infantry, under Colonel Ulysses Grant McAlexander, to hold a line from Varennes and the valley of the River Surmelin to the south, and along the Marne to Mézy, where the river turns west. To their left were the 30th Infantry, the 7th Infantry, opposite Gland, and the 4th Infantry, all with the bulk of their troops well back from the river. Degoutte, however, did not approve of a deployment that placed so few troops on the riverbank; the Americans should, he insisted, receive the Germans with 'one foot in the water'. The American units therefore made an appearance of compliance, before resuming their former positions when the

Frenchman had departed. The penetration anticipated by the Germans was considerable, as the map captured by the 3rd Division shows.

In the air the Americans were starting to make themselves felt. The American First Pursuit Group, formed of the 94th, 95th, 27th and 147th Squadrons, had moved to this sector at the end of June and became virtually the only Allied air presence during the fighting on the Marne. On 14 July they had observed the build-up of German forces. On the same day, Quentin Roosevelt, the youngest son of former President Theodore Roosevelt, newly qualified as a pilot, was shot down and killed near Chamery.

The French and American artillery beat the Germans to the punch just before midnight. The gathering Germans were hit before their own barrage started and the first minutes of 15 July were filled with the flash and crash of the guns of both sides. Colonel

Right **Wounded of the 30th and 38th Infantry receiving first aid from No. 5 Ambulance Company at Courboin, west of Condé-en-Brie, 15 July 1918.**
(USAMHI/ASC 17341) [4/24]

William Mitchell took to the air in his Nieuport XXVIII and flew low along the river, where he saw the pontoons and German troops deployed in readiness for the crossing. Orders were given for the bombing and strafing of the crossings. On the right the French were quick to fall back, but the detachments of the 28th Division with them were, through some failure of communication, left isolated to fight on and die or become prisoners. Colonel McAlexander had foreseen the collapse of his support on the right flank and his F Company was facing east on the ridge overlooking Reuilly. They were supported to the south, in the Bois de Condé, by part of the retreating French division – to be precise, the Pennsylvanians of 109th Infantry, US 28th Division.

In 17th-century warfare it was the custom to break up enemy attacks by placing a small force forward of the main body of the army. Membership of this force was an honour, and survival was doubtful. It is no wonder that these bodies of men were called 'The Forlorn Hope'. The forlorn hope of Captain Jesse W. Wooldridge's G Company was the platoon commanded by Lieutenant Calkins on the river bank (see map, square U20). The rest of the company was behind the railway line overlooking the wheatfield that lay between them. To their right, up towards Varennes, H and E Companies adopted similar dispositions. At 1am the Germans had their pontoon boats afloat and crossing, only to run into heavy automatic fire from the opposite bank. It was not until an hour had passed and countless men had been lost to bullet and grenade, that the Germans finally overcame Wooldridge's forlorn hope. Lieutenant Calkins was wounded but survived. By 7am

three German companies had established a bridgehead on the railway embankment at Mézy. By 8am the 38th Infantry had destroyed them with a wild charge.

The unexpected resistance of the Americans would surely crumble under the attack of the crack troops of the German Guards Division. Two regiments were sent across the Marne against the 38th Infantry as dawn broke, gained the bank and worked forward through the wheatfield. The fighting broke into a confused pattern of small units of Americans who refused to yield, shooting, bayoneting and bombing the elite forces attacking them. As the day drew on, McAlexander ordered supporting troops forward. Billy Mitchell's airmen, joined by two French squadrons of Breguet XIVs, machine-gunned troops attempting to cross the river and dropped 10-kg and 20-kg bombs (45 tons of them in all) on their pontoon bridges. By nightfall the Germans could claim no more than a fingerhold on the southern bank in the American sector.

Mitchell brought new pressure to bear on the Germans the following day. In answer to his call, four RAF squadrons of DH9 day bombers from the British 9 Brigade raided the German supply dumps at Fère-en-Tardenois, escorted by two squadrons of SE5As, two of Sopwith Camels and by US First Pursuit Group. The German airmen rallied to the defence, shooting down 12 British bombers, but left their forward troops at the mercy of other Allied aircraft. The 7,500 German troops south of the Marne, mostly in the French sector, were pushed back over the next three days. The US 3rd Division had earned themselves the honorific title of 'The Rock of the Marne'.

THE TIDE TURNS

Below **The 5th Marines, 2nd
Division, between Montreuil
and Château-Thierry on the
move to the Soissons front.**
(USAMHI/ASC 14675) [4/11]

By the end of June the AEF had more than a million men in France, but every division in the line was under the command of either the British or the French. Around the Marne Salient, bulging south to Château-Thierry from the Soissons-Reims line along the River Vesle, was gathered the nucleus of an army in the shape of six American divisions: the 2nd, 3rd, 4th, 26th, 28th and 42nd. General Pershing argued that the American Army should now come into being, and Foch proved receptive to the proposal that it should take over a line in the east. Pershing pushed for Lorraine, the original plan, in accordance with which much work had been done to build lines of supply. Foch favoured the Argonne, west of Verdun, to create three great commands with the British in the north, the French in the centre and the Americans in the east, leaving the extreme east quiet. Before either course could be adopted, however, there was unfinished business in the Marne Salient.

Ludendorff's five great offensives had pushed two huge dents in the Allies' lines and it was vital to reduce both of them. With their attempt on the Marne stalled,

the Germans were ripe for a crushing blow. Foch planned to hit them first on the western flank, south of Soissons, and then in the south, driving up from the Marne. The Soissons operation was entrusted to the energetic and aggressive General Mangin, using his French Tenth Army's XX Corps, which consisted of the US 1st Division, the 1st Moroccan Division and the US 2nd Division. Major-General Charles P. Summerall now had command of the 1st, and Harbord, now himself a major-general, had command of the 2nd Division. A week before the attack, neither force was anywhere near their start line and they had to make a hasty approach through the Forest of Retz astride the Paris-Soissons road (now the N2). On the evening of 17 July they were still making their way up for the next day's surprise attack.

Major Raymond Austin, 6th Field Artillery, 1st Division, wrote to his mother at Ohio Wesleyan University on 31 July:

We were relieved [from the Mondidier line] at midnight about 7 July... We marched all night... We put in three more long night marches... I saw many a driver asleep in the saddle and at every halt men would drop sound asleep on the ground or leaning against trees... [I] got dull in thought and action, and the last night I began to 'see things'. Distant objects like stars, lights, lone trees, etc. would move back and forth and the road would seem to creep like the track when you look at it from the end of a train... When I reached Crépy [-en-Valois] I began to realize the immensity of the operation that was about to commence. Truck trains in endless numbers moved along every road, batteries of light artillery, immense tractor-drawn 6-, 8- and 12-inch guns, staff cars hastening in all directions, blue snake-like columns of French infantry, regiments of Senegalese troops, brown-skinned Moroccans in olive drab uniforms similar to ours, groups of Indo-Chinese laborers, strangely camouflaged tanks, military police at all turns and crossroads directing traffic, like policemen in a big city... The entire distance from Mortefontaine to Cœuvres [-et-Valsery] was one solid mass of tanks, ammunition trains, trucks, infantry and artillery.

The infantry had a hard time of it. Private Francis of the 5th Marines, 2nd Division, wrote:

At dusk [on 17 July] we started our hike, which proved to be one of the hardest the 2nd Division ever undertook, if

'I never realized that there was that much artillery in the world...'

not the hardest ever undertaken by any AEF troops. It was raining and we were tired and hungry. We were forbidden to eat our emergency rations. The road was narrow and literally overrun with equipment going to the lines. I know Broadway never saw such a night for congestion; it was impossible to

see two feet in front of us... The last five miles we had to double time all the way to the jumping-off place. In the meantime I had such a pain over my heart that I had to drop out for an hour and rest for I was hiking practically doubled over, but I managed to catch my outfit just at the Zero hour, at 4am.

Second Lieutenant John D. Clark, 15th Field Artillery, 2nd Division, saw the infantry coming up.

...There seemed to be a darker shadow approaching and I reined in the horse just in time to avoid running into a column of infantrymen who were dog-trotting in the mud with each man holding onto the shoulder of the man in front of him. They were to reach the front just in time to shed their packs and go over the top.

SOISSONS

Coming up from the south the Soissons–Château-Thierry road runs past Villemontoire, Buzancy and Berzy-le-Sec, along the edge of the plateau that stretches to the west. The high flatland is cut by numerous steep little valleys in which the fortified villages of Vierzy, Ploisy and Missy-aux-Bois formed forward defences for the towns that dominated the main road. It was towards this road that the Allies launched themselves behind a creeping barrage in the dawn of 18 July. Major Austin wrote:

I never realized that there was that much artillery in the world... The infantry went forward in a long line extending as far as could be seen to either side, the successive waves following each other at intervals... My PC and that of the 16th Infantry were in a trench on a high ridge on the forward side of Cœvres, just across the town and valley from my batteries... I studied out on the map an approximate advance position to which I could take the battalion as soon as the infantry had advanced far enough into German territory... When the 16th had reached its third objective of the first day, I started out... [They] had advanced as far as the range of our guns would permit us to support them and it had become necessary to move the guns forward... We had changed from the stereotyped trench warfare to a warfare of manoeuvre...

The 1st Division's progress was swift at first but the German artillery soon responded and the wheatfields proved to be peppered with German machine-gun nests. In the south the 2nd Division pushed forward to the edge of the Vierzy ravine. William Francis said:

Our advance for the first few miles was nothing but a hike... Late in the evening we had orders to take a town on our right which was very large and was quite a railroad center. We had to wade through a swamp over our waists, and immediately beyond was the town of Vierzy. We had to go up a steep embankment; we crawled to the top and the Germans opened up, but we couldn't find their machine-guns. We finally noticed that they were firing from the top of

'They dropped wonderfully brilliant illuminating shells that hung in the air...'

the buildings and we dislodged them, and also got one out of a tree... On our left was a big prairie. I watched the rest of the boys go over with tanks and cavalry. It was a beautiful sight to see the French with their long lances go after the Germans... The night of the 18th was freezing cold. I was soaking wet from wading in the swamp. Gas shells were falling all around so we had to sleep with our gas masks on.

Francis makes it sound easier than it was. The lack of an interval between arrival and attack left the 2nd Division's communications in complete confusion, and the taking of Vierzy was a very muddled affair. Nonetheless, they had advanced nearly four and a half miles in the day.

In the centre the progress of the Moroccans was checked by strong resistance, but they had still managed to push forward more than three miles, while the 1st Division on their left had been held back by the poor performance of the French 153rd Division to their north. Heavy fire from Missy-aux-Bois had held them up for a while but their day's progress was three miles. As night fell Raymond Austin was at Missy-aux-Bois working out positions for his artillery the following day. He was shocked by the suffering of the wounded.

The ambulance service didn't work very well the first day. The road between Croix-le-Fer and Missy-aux-Bois was thickly lined with wounded, tagged (name, injury and first-aid treatment) awaiting transportation. Many died there before they could be got to the dressing stations... That surely was a bad night. The big [German] bombing planes would fly low over us, escorted by small fast fighting planes... they dropped wonderfully brilliant illuminating shells that hung in the air... then... they dropped heavy bombs that burst with terrific concussions... I have never felt so helpless in my life...

At 4am on 19 July the Allied attack continued. The objective was to cross the north-south road, the 1st Division north of Buzancy, the 2nd around Hartennes. Neither of them made it. The Germans had taken command of the skies. The crack Jagdgeschwader 1 (a Jagdgeschwader consisted of several Jastas), Richthofen's 'Flying Circus' (although its leader had become a fatal casualty on the Somme in April, and it was now commanded by the young Hermann Göring) was more than a match for the inexperienced pilots of the US First Pursuit Group. Overnight artillery and

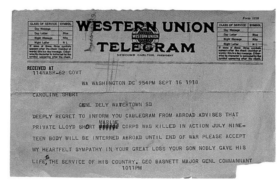

machine-gun reinforcements had stiffened the German lines and two fresh divisions had been brought up. The US 1st Division was again hampered by the failure of the French 153rd Division to clear the Missy-aux-Bois ravine, and the supporting tanks were halted by the Ploisy ravine. As the day wore on the situation became increasingly confused and the 1st had to postpone its efforts until some semblance of organisation could be recreated. Sergeant Earl R. Poorbaugh, 26th Infantry, who had until then enjoyed the luxury of liaison duties because of his ability to speak French, thus avoiding menial tasks, was pinned down by machine-gun fire.

As was my usual custom, I had discarded my pack, retaining only my cartridge belt, gas mask and pistol, knowing that I could always find an entrenching tool carried by some unfortunate comrade who would have no further use for it. However, on this day the only thing I could find was a messkit lid and I was really making the dirt fly with this improvised shovel when Major [Theodore] Roosevelt [eldest of the four sons of former President Teddy Roosevelt who served in France] crept up beside me and inquired, with his usual grin, 'What's the matter, Poorbaugh, did you forget how to speak French?' I didn't even slow down – I just kept digging. Major Roosevelt was later wounded, as I also was, and purely by chance we went to the Evacuation Hospital in the same ambulance. Between us we had one cigarette which we shared.

Major Austin was on the move, seeking new positions for his guns.

I heard a lot of noise which I mistook, at first, for the chirping of sparrows... [it] proved to be made by the bullets of a machine-gun barrage going over our heads... We went on to the crest and took cover beside a disabled tank... Through the big shell hole torn in its side the 75 [-mm] gun, the same size as our field guns, was visible. Hanging over it and lying beside it were the bodies of the crew. They must have been instantly killed by the shell... While I was waiting for [the battery] to come up, Major Roosevelt was brought to the road slightly wounded in the leg, and, when the battery limbers went back, I put him on one and sent him to the rear.

The 2nd Division had an equally tough day. The Moroccans between the 1st and the 2nd kept pace with the former, but their right made poorer progress, leaving the 2nd exposed. William Francis experienced the result with the 5th Marines.

About dusk, the Germans began flanking us on our left with artillery. One shell hit in a dugout and carried away our lieutenant... They found one of his limbs about one hundred yards from his dugout. Now the Germans were killing lots of the boys. The company on our left lost practically all their men.

What Francis does not say is that they had fought their way across the wheatfields to the outskirts of Tigny, just short of their objective. The cost had been

high, the 2nd Division reporting casualties of 3,788 men. They were relieved that night by the French 58th Colonial Division, with which the 15th Field Artillery stayed in support. John Clark was making ready to move the guns forward as the Algerians advanced.

...We proceeded according to plan and had just pulled out on the road when Major Bailey galloped back and yelled, 'Get back in there and resume firing. Those god-damned sons o'bitches are not advancing. They're retreating'... That day each of our guns fired a thousand rounds. The gun barrels got so hot that we were firing three of them and pouring water over the other one... By the end of the day we had halted the infantry retreat... The Algerians were reputed to be ferocious soldiers on attack but they were not very reliable on defense... But the Algerians, assisted by fresh French troops, held... Finally, on July 25th, we were relieved...

Above **Waiting for the order to attack a machine-gun nest, men of the 16th Infantry rest in a ravine near Berzy-le-Sec.** (USAMHI/ASC 16487) [1/14]

Below **On the plateau west of Ploisy a 155-mm howitzer battery of the 1st Division moves into forward positions to support the attack at Berzy-le-Sec.** (USAMHI/ASC 176670) [3/22]

For the 1st Division the battle was not over. They fought on for two more days, finally crossing the Château-Thierry road and occupying the heights north of the River Crise, dominating the town of Soissons. During the night of 22–23 July they were relieved by the British 15th (Scottish) Division, having lost nearly 1,000 killed out of a total 7,000 casualties. For Major-General Harbord the aftermath must have been a disappointment. Pershing, with the formation of the American Army in prospect, needed the Services of Supply operating at a level of supreme efficiency; Harbord was offered the task and loyally accepted. Brigadier-General John A. Lejeune assumed command of the 2nd Division.

THE OURCQ

The failure of the Germans against the 3rd Division south of the Marne coincided with the opening of the Allied offensive at Soissons. The Germans immediately started to withdraw from the southern side of the Marne Salient and on 21 July the 3rd crossed the river. The Germans were pulling back along the road from Jaulgonne north towards the valley of the River Ourcq. It was a fighting retreat designed to permit the recovery of the massive supplies they had gathered to support their recent offensive. The 3rd Division forced them out of the village of Le Charmel on 25 July. On the night of 26–27 July the enemy moved back again to a line on the Ourcq and prepared to make a stand.

On 28 July the 28th Division were in the line at Courmont, overlooking the broad valley of the Ourcq, on the 3rd's left, while the 42nd (Rainbow) Division stood on the 28th's left on a line looped around the village of Villers-sur-Fère, approximately along the modern D6 road. The same day, on the Soissons–Château-Thierry road, all the heights to the east fell into the hands of the Allies.

The German choice of line was, as usual, well made. The Ourcq runs from Ronchères north-west to Fère-en-Tardenois, east of which, towards Seringes, rises Hill 184. Halfway along that length of the river, and on the far side from where the Americans were, is the village of Sergy, south-east of which is Hill 212. These hills dominate the valley. The river itself was swollen by rain to a depth of eight feet and a width of 40 feet. The bridges were down. The three American divisions advanced to force a crossing early in the morning of 28 July. The 3rd Division's 4th Infantry had little difficulty in taking Ronchères, but the 28th Division was delayed by a faulty relief of the French 39th Division which was late in sending guides. As a result, the sun was up before they could move. They ran into fierce fire from La Motte Farm and did not bridge the river before 3pm.

Once across, the German fire from Hill 212 and the Bois des Grimpettes, north of Ronchères, pinned them down only a quarter of a mile from the riverbank and they were forced to dig in.

The 42nd went forward to meet heavy fire from Sergy and Meurcy Farm from which they recoiled at first, but they were over the river by 10.30am. Here, German spotter aircraft directed artillery fire on them from batteries on the southern edge of the Forêt de Nesles. Their foothold in the outskirts of Sergy was battered by fire from Hill 212 and the woods of les Jomblets and la Planchette which crowned it. A counterattack by the German 4th Guards Division threw them out of the village, but a fresh attack got the Americans back in the western fringes of Sergy.

Below **The plan of attack on the Ourcq. On the left US I Corps (42nd, 26th and 4th Divisions) and on the right US XXXVIII Corps (3rd, 32nd and 28th Divisions) with assumed positions for 28 July and axes of advance.** (USAMHI/MFME MF 2/5)

'Shells, high-explosives, were bursting all around us and it was pitiful to see the sights.'

All day attack and counter-attack saw the village change hands until, at about 8pm, the 42nd managed to establish themselves in at least part of it. Corporal Norman L. Summers, 167th Infantry, was not in action until the afternoon.

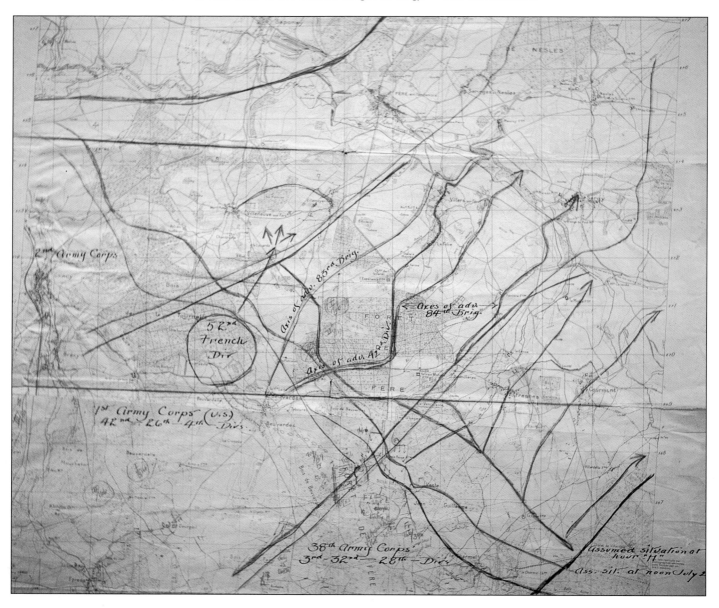

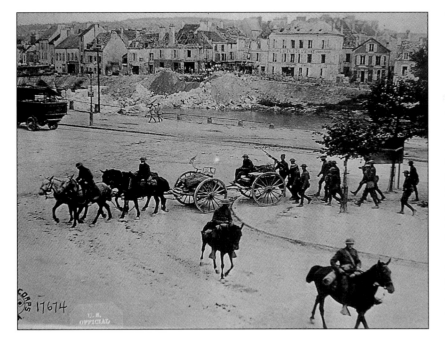

Above **The ruins of the bridge over the Marne and the shattered houses of Château-Thierry, 25 July 1918. Men of 150th Field Artillery, 42nd Division, a machine-gun mounted on a cart for anti-aircraft defence, move towards the Ourcq.** (USAMHI/ASC 17674) [6/9]

Above, right **The American Battle Monuments Commission Oise-Aisne Cemetery between Fère-en-Tardenois and Nesles, on ground won by the 42nd Division in 1918. The graves of 6,012 men are here, and the names of 241 more with no known graves are recorded on the walls of the chapel.** (MFME Yp/Ar 7/27)

Below right **The memorial to Quentin Roosevelt at Chamery.** (MFME Yp/Ar 7/23)

We dug small holes which very much resembled graves. These afforded protection from shells unless one bursted over us. At 5pm we received orders to advance. We started thru a heavy counter-barrage by the Germans. Shells, high-explosives, were bursting all around us and it was pitiful to see the sights. Some of our men were blown to pieces, some had their legs or arms blown into tatters. Dead horses were lying everywhere and the stench was awful. Dead Americans, French and Germans were lying everywhere... The Germans tried to flank us on our left but were soon discouraged as our machine-guns and rifle fire would leave a line of dead as they advanced. We were up against the Prussian Guards, the best soldiers Germany has, but we were more than holding our own with them. In this ditch I was gassed. I could hardly get my breath and everything seemed to go round and round.

Raiding parties from both sides harried each other through the night. As the next morning broke, the

'Dead Americans, French and Germans were lying everywhere...'

Germans' heavy bombardment and a determined attack by the 4th Guards drove the Americans out of Sergy once more. The whole 42nd Division struck back, both at Sergy and also at Meurcy Farm and Seringes-et-Nesles on the left. Sergy was in American hands by noon, as were the other objectives, including Hill 184, by the end of a day of desperate fighting. On their right the 3rd Division had made no progress north of Ronchères against Meunière Wood. The exhausted unit was relieved by the 32nd Division that night, while the battered 42nd was reinforced by two battalions of the 47th Infantry, 4th Division. All through the night German shelling pounded the American lines.

The 28th Division succeeded in reaching the outskirts of Cierges and the 32nd in clearing Gimpettes Wood. The 28th was now exhausted by two weeks of fighting and the 32nd took over, extending its line to the left alongside the 42nd. The battle ground on with the Americans making repeated attacks, winning small gains and stubbornly refusing to yield under constant German shell and machine-gun fire and in the face of persistent counter-attacks. Then, on 1 August, the German fire slackened. They had been pushed out of their principal positions facing the River Ourcq and had no choice but to withdraw. The battle-scarred 42nd Division was relieved by the 4th, which, with the 32nd, moved forward against minor resistance from the retreating German forces. On taking Chamery on 2 August the 32nd found Quentin Roosevelt's grave; their officers had to prevent too many soldiers visiting it, as the pursuit of the enemy was a top priority. By 6 August they were on the River Vesle at Fismes. The great salient had at last been regained.

Above **Snipers of the 166th
Infantry, 42nd Division, in
action at Villers-sur-Fère.**
(USAMHI/ASC 18672) [5/8]

Below, right **Australian troops
clearing the Amiens-Roye
railway, with a Mark V tank in
support, 8 August 1918.**
(TM 64/H2)

> **'Hurry, here
> comes the
> king.'
> 'What king?'
> 'George
> King.'**

The cost for both sides in the battles of 15 July to 5 August had been heavy. The Allies suffered 160,852 killed, wounded and missing. Of these the greatest burden was borne by the French: 95,165 casualties. The British total came to some 16,000, the Italian to 9,334, and the American to 40,353. German losses totalled some 168,000, of whom 29,367 were prisoners. With the German divisions from the former Russian front expended, such a loss could not be made good. And for Ludendorff's armies worse was to come.

THE BLACK DAY

In conference with Field Marshal Haig and General Pershing on 24 July, General Foch proposed the next strategic objectives: the elimination of the salients at Amiens and St-Mihiel. American manpower had now made the Allied forces the equal of the German, and the continuing flow across the Atlantic would soon give them superiority. On the same day Pershing issued the order for the creation of the American First Army, to take effect on 10 August.

The Amiens Salient was dealt with on 8 August. With the Amiens-Roye road as the axis of attack, four Australian divisions on the left and four Canadian divisions on the right were to make the assault. North of them, over the River Somme, the British III Corps would secure the left flank while the French First Army would hold the right flank. Tanks were to play a key part. There were 324 Mark V heavy tanks, supported by 184 supply tanks; in addition, two battalions of Whippet light tanks would also take part. The heavy artillery numbered nearly 700 pieces and there were twice that number of field guns. The Royal Air Force was there with the greater part of its strength, some 800 aircraft, while the French Armée de l'air contributed an even larger number. On 6 August, however, the British were taken by surprise when the Germans attacked the Chipilly Spur, north of the Somme. Pushed back, their preparations for the coming battle were disrupted. Yet

Above **A massive German artillery piece, of the type known to allied troops as 'Big Bertha', at Cappy-sur-Somme. It was intended for the shelling of Amiens and was taken by men of the 33rd Division on 9 August.**
(USAMHI/ASC 25211) [7/8]

advance. The British 58th Division was reinforced by the 131st Infantry of the US 33rd Division on 9 August for the recovery of the Chipilly Spur and Gressaire Wood. The assault began at 5.30pm and by nightfall, with the help of the Australian 4th Division coming over the river from the south, the spur itself and half the wood were taken. Corporal Jake Allex, 131st Infantry, took over command of his platoon when the officers were wounded and, finding his men pinned down by machine-gun fire, worked his way forward to the German strongpoint. Having killed five men with his bayonet, the weapon broke, so he reversed arms and clubbed the remaining 15 into surrender. He was awarded the Congressional Medal of Honor. The 33rd remained in the area long enough to be recognised, congratulated and have some of their number decorated by King George V on 12 August. Will Judy witnessed the ceremony.

At eleven on this sunny morning the heralds came up the hill and soon the royal car shone in the sunlight as it moved between the two rows of poplars that for a quarter-mile border the road to the chateau at the top of the hill. An American soldier near me rushed back and called to his comrade: 'Hurry, here comes the king.'

'What king?'

'George King.'

We crowded the sidewalks, silent in expectancy. The long limousine, black and sleek, drew near and one American called out loudly – 'So that's the big stiff!'

King George V of England led the procession to the green back of the chateau. General Pershing walked on his left; then came General Bliss, General [Sir] Henry Rawlinson [commanding British Fourth Army] and General Bell [Major-General George Bell, Jr, commanding 33rd Division], and after them a host, including myself. About twenty officers and men of the 131st and 132nd Infantry stood at attention. The movie cameras clicked, the king pinned an English medal on each, the band played 'God Save the King', and then the 'Star-Spangled Banner'; the procession returned to the chateau, the band played 'Illinois', and the little white-bellied donkey that wanders around our headquarters every day, stood nearby half-asleep thru it all, ready to kick King George in the rear side as readily as a soldier of the ranks.

in spite of this potential threat to the Australian advance the battle commenced as scheduled at 4.20am on 8 August.

In what the Australians were to describe as '*a très bon stunt*' they and the Canadians advanced a minimum of six and a maximum of eight miles that day, pausing mainly to ensure contact with their support and supplies. On the northern flank the Australian progress was slowed by flanking fire from the Germans and action had to be taken by III Corps to free them for a further

Then the division left to join the American First Army in the east.

Ludendorff described 8 August as 'the black day of the German Army'. He had lost 30,000 men and in the days following would lose more as the British made inexorable progress over the ground lost the previous March and April. In seven weeks the initiative had passed irretrievably from the Germans to the Allies.

THE AMERICAN BATTLE

General Pershing visited Field Marshal Haig on 12 August and demanded the return of the five divisions which were training and serving under British command. Haig took the request badly, but gave in to it. Although Pershing's mission to create the American First Army and reduce the St-Mihiel Salient had already been accepted, Haig thought it unwise to weaken a force which was rolling the enemy back in Picardy. Marshal Foch (as he had become) intervened, persuading Pershing to leave the 27th and 30th Divisions with the British. In addition, the 33rd, 78th and 80th were to be left for the build-up in the east.

Also in August, the AEF ceased training with the French and British entirely, taking full responsibility for raising their troops to combat readiness. It would soon be the case that virtually the only US troops serving under French command were the black regiments of the 93rd Division.

Allied pressure on the Germans was maintained when, on 20 August, Mangin hurled them back to the Oise. The following day Haig hit them north of the tortured countryside over which the first Battle of the Somme had been fought. The retreat to the prepared positions of the Hindenburg Line was taking place for a second time. All thought of the decisive blow against the British in Flanders was abandoned. Against the

Hindenburg Line, of course, the open warfare so joyfully welcomed by the Americans would be impossible.

On 29 August Pershing established the headquarters of the American First Army at Ligny-en-Barrois, 25 miles south-east of St-Mihiel, and started work on the takeover of the Lorraine front. No sooner had this task been taken in hand, however, than the basic concept was changed. Foch presented Pershing with a plan to reduce a larger salient than ever before – the entire German front line between Verdun and Ypres. This line was supported by the railway from Strasbourg which passed to the north of the River Meuse. If the Americans could strike up through the Argonne Forest, the line could be severed in the region of Sedan and Mézières, leaving the Germans reliant on supply lines through Belgium alone. That the railway might have been more vulnerable further east was not considered, and it must be said that the concept of the three great Allied armies advancing shoulder to shoulder had its attractions. If this chance to end the war in 1918 was to be seized, operations had to start by early October

Right **The Tranchée de la Soif, the 'Trench of Thirst', in the Bois d'Apremont on the hills above St-Mihiel, where the French heroically contested the German advance in 1914.** (MFME Yp/Ar 5/17)

Below **The graves of French fallen lie below the Crête des Éparges.** (MFME Yp/Ar 6/13)

before the winter weather endangered their completion. Before that Pershing had to wipe out the St-Mihiel Salient, and then assemble his forces to take up the battle miles away to the north-west. It was a very tall order indeed, but Pershing agreed, albeit with deep misgivings.

ST-MIHIEL

After the German invasion had been halted on the Marne in 1914, renewed attempts were made to outflank the French at Verdun by taking the Meuse Heights. The river runs south from Verdun and the heights lie to the east, terminating just south of St-Mihiel, and east of them the plain of the Woevre stretches away to Metz. In the last days of September the Germans seized the southern part of the heights and crossed the Meuse, only to be forced back to St-Mihiel by the French XVI Corps. This left a salient through Combres in the north, Chauvoncourt, across the river from St-Mihiel, in the west, and through Apremont and Seicheprey and along the hills above the valley of the River Rupt de Mad in the south. The presence of the Germans here was a constant threat to Verdun. French efforts against the salient were directed against the northern flank, following a failed attack at Chauvoncourt in November 1914. The eminence of Les Éparges was gained on 9 April 1915. The line then remained stable — if the constant raiding, mining and counter-mining merit that word — and out of the front line the Germans enjoyed a measure of tranquillity.

Two ideas influenced the American approach to the reduction of the salient: secrecy and efficiency. The gathering of the First Army was to be concealed from the enemy as far as was possible. The operation was to be the acid test of the army's abilities — not of the fighting spirit of its men, for this was now beyond doubt, but of organisation and staff work. The staff were under the direction of Captain Hugh Drum, First Army Chief of Staff, and Colonel George C. Marshall, Jr., on loan from AEF headquarters (later to become General of the Army, and the man who had overall command of the US Army during the Second World War). They were responsible for the assembly of 550,000 American soldiers, 110,000 French, 3,010 guns, 40,000 tons of ammunition, 267 tanks and 65 evacuation trains. In support, Colonel Mitchell was gathering an air force of unprecedented size. He had 609 American aircraft at his disposal, of which 108 were US-built Liberty DH4s, and with the contributions made by the French, British and Italians, he assembled a force of 696 fighters, 366 reconnaissance aircraft, 323 day bombers and 91 night bombers. With 20 observation balloons, the air fleet numbered 1,496 craft.

Second Lieutenant Clark of the 15th Field Artillery was among the men making ready. On 8 September he wrote:

After three night marches we are now bivouaced just behind the front line near Toul, waiting to pull into position and open up on the hour 'H', for the attack seems imminent. From what I see and hear, the preparations are extensive; our entire division occupies a front of only one kilometer — which indicates that the troops are heavily massed...That the Boche know we are here is very evident, for yesterday a balloon message came over, which read, 'To the 9th Infantry — we know you are here and we are — ready for you.' I really feel sorry for them, because if they are ready for the Ninth, or any others of our division, as they say, they must have made their wills and resigned themselves either to death or a prison camp. For our motto is 'Let's go!' and no Boche obstacles have stopped us yet.

Private Francis of the 5th Marines, also in the 2nd Division, described the approach to the front.

We camped about ten miles back of the Front for about eight days, in dense woods. It rained every day... We finally received orders to move to the Front. Although it was raining, we hiked all night,

Below **American soldiers, 1918. Left, a mechanic of the 79th Division with a Springfield rifle; centre, a first sergeant of the 88th with a semi-automatic pistol and, right, a captain of artillery, 83rd Division, wearing the Sam Browne belt beloved of Pershing and hated by others. The shoulder insignia were, at this time, unstandardized and often not worn at all.** (Osprey, MAA 230 *US Army 1890-1920*) (Jeffrey Burn)

Above **The front to be attacked by the 26th Division in the Bois des Éparges, 10 September 1918.** (USAMHI/ASC 23457) [6/30]

Below **Bangalore torpedoes, tubes packed with cheddite explosive, were used to blow up enemy barbed wire. Here they are being taken forward by the 307th Engineers, 82nd Division, for an attack at Choloy, 1 August 1918.** (USAMHI/ASC 18770) [4/31]

and the morning found us in the front line waiting for Zero hour. We were standing in three feet of water.

The French were facing the tip of the salient at St-Mihiel, while lined out along the southern side were the US 1st, 42nd, 89th, 2nd, 5th, 90th and 82nd Divisions. The eastern face of the salient was mainly the province of the French, with the exception of the American 26th Division. The 1st and 42nd Divisions from the south and the 26th from the west were to drive towards, and meet at, Vigneulles, trapping as many Germans as possible in the nose of the salient. The rest of the attacking forces were to push towards the Michel Line, the fortified position which the Germans had built at the back of the salient.

The attackers faced multiple lines of barbed wire and trenches. The 89th and 5th Divisions would also have to clear tangled woods. It was known that an assault on prepared positions like these required the destruction of the barbed wire either by shellfire,

Bangalore torpedoes (explosive charges contained in long tubes) or by tanks, which were also the key to overcoming the defenders' machine-guns. George Patton, by now a lieutenant-colonel and commander of the Tank Corps, was anxious to ensure that his tanks performed impeccably in the coming battle. He made a night reconnaissance with a French officer to inspect the tank route. The light Renault tanks with which Patton's corps was equipped had little weight of armour, relying more on speed – a dizzy six miles per hour – than brute force to gain their objectives. Although he satisfied himself that the ground was firm, and having had the curious experience of hearing a German whistle to warn him off when he got too close, instead of shooting him, the plans were changed and another route was chosen. The reconnaissance had to be done again, this time under shellfire. The last of Patton's tanks was detrained at 3am, with 'H' hour only two hours off. He issued his orders, adding:

No tank is to be surrendered or abandoned to the enemy. If you are left alone in the midst of the enemy keep shooting. If your gun is disabled use your pistols and squash the enemy with your tracks... [A tank's] presence will save the lives of hundreds of infantry and kill many Germans...

Corporal Rudolph A. Forderhase, 356th Infantry, 89th Division, was a drafted man. He later wrote that, 'except for a few gung-ho people the great majority could not see the need to go to Europe to fight a war.' But he went on to say, 'Although of German descent, I felt it my duty to do what I could for my country.' Now he was in the village of Flirey, preparing for battle.

We were ordered to make up combat packs (we rolled up our blankets, extra pair of shoes, tent pole and stakes, in our shelter half). Each man was issued with two extra bandoleers of ammunition. We hated these... [one] was slung over each shoulder... to bring so much pressure on both sides of the neck... was torture. We were checked and rechecked for not only ammunition, but grenades, intrenching tools, first-aid kit and rations... I was aroused by the Platoon

Sergeant, at midnight... a light rain was falling. It was so dark, and the rain made the footing so treacherous, that every man held on to the man ahead of him in order to avoid falling or straggling. We soon entered a communicating trench where the footing was no better. Suddenly the artillery began to shell the German positions we were about to attack.

It was 1am on 12 September. The bombardment continued for four hours, and then the men moved forward. Raymond Austin wrote home:

The infantry went over at the appointed time, appearing as a line miles long moving slowly forward, followed at intervals by succeeding waves, the later waves being broken up into small squads instead of being in continuous long lines, as the telephone squads running wires, engineers, stretcher bearers, etc. advanced. It was a great sight, that broad expanse of country dotted everywhere with men and tanks, bursting shells, rockets rising and bursting into white, red, green stars, Mont Sec looming up dark and forbidding and showing here and there on its sides white puffs of smoke which told where our big 8-inch guns were dropping their shells — all in the gray light of early morning under the broken storm clouds against which the fast, low-flying airplanes were sharply silhouetted.

Billy Mitchell's air war was going well. The night before the attack, massive British Handley Page O/400 bombers had hit Metz and Thionville, while the French bombers attacked targets within the salient. French squadrons and the American Second Pursuit Group flew strafing missions in support of the infantry, while 103rd Squadron of the Third Pursuit Group bombed transport and troop concentrations. Deeper into the salient the French flew bombing missions alternately from north and south. The American First Pursuit Group swept down from the north, only 100 feet above the ground, to smash the German aircraft attempting to combat the total domination of the air which Mitchell

had achieved. It was to be another two days before the Germans could gather themselves sufficiently to challenge the Americans and their allies in the sky.

Corporal Forderhase was ready to go.

The order to advance came at full daylight. The rain had made the clay muddy and slick. The shorter men had some difficulty getting out of the trench that was about four feet deep, but the willing hands of the taller men were helpful. We formed squads, in single file, to start across no-mansland. The enemy could not see us at first. When he did, we were greeted by both machine-gun and rifle fire. We dived into a large shell crater. I was unable to locate the gun. Almost instantly it stopped firing at us. I ordered the men to form, on either side of me, at intervals of 20 feet and we

Above **H Company, 167th Infantry, 42nd Division, ready to move into attack. Two of these men were killed by artillery fire five minutes after this picture was taken.**
(USAMHI/ACS 25318) [5/23]

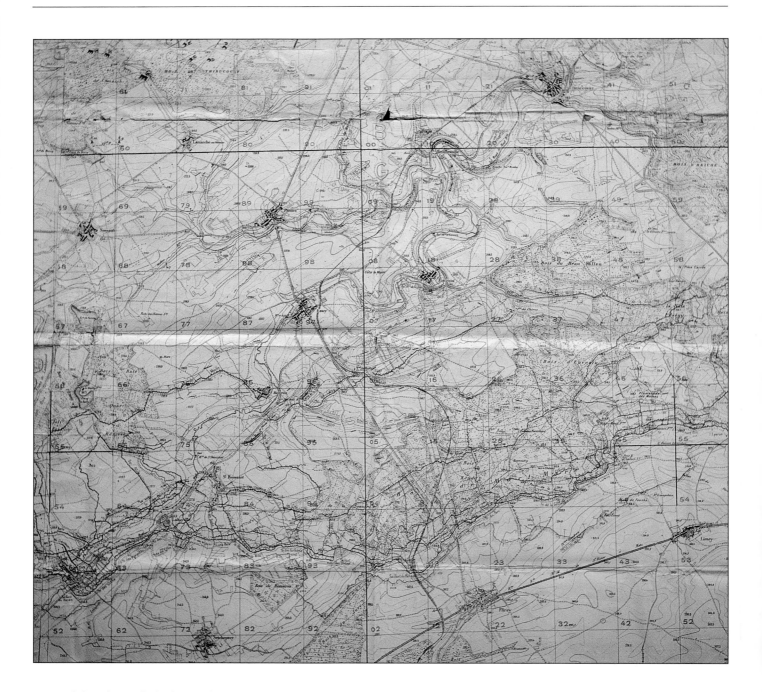

continued the advance. *Evidently our advancing troops had overrun the gun that had fired on us. By the time we reached the main German trench their resistance had ceased.*

Only one of Forderhase's men had been wounded, a slight flesh wound below the knee. He was sent to a dressing station, but never made it; one of the few German shells fired that day killed him on the way.

The tanks of 304th Battalion, US Tank Corps, were operating in support of the 42nd Division and George Patton was following on foot. When he outran the length of the telephone line that had been laid he went forward with a team of four runners to carry messages.

Hearing that his tanks had halted in front of the village of Essey he hurried forward, striding along smoking his pipe as much, he said, to keep up his own courage as to give confidence to the men. A yet more exposed position on a small hill was occupied by an American officer. Climbing up, Patton found Brigadier-General Douglas MacArthur, Chief of Staff of the 42nd, coolly viewing the battle. The tanks had stopped, it emerged, because they feared that the bridge into Essey had been mined by the enemy. Patton, 'in a catlike manner, expecting to be blown to heaven any moment', walked across it, and the tanks followed.

Right **The build-up of the American First Army around the St-Mihiel Salient. Situation on 10 September, 1918, as shown on the secret G-3 map No. 1405.** (USAMHI/MFME 7/19)

Left **The southern sector of the St-Mihiel Salient showing German trenches (blue) as at 20 March 1918 and the American front line (red). On this front the 1st Division were on the left, to advance towards Nonsard (square F58), the 42nd in the centre to advance on a front centred on Pannes (square F88) and the 89th on the right, pushing for Bouillonville (square G19).**
(USAMHI/Chambley/MFME MF 1/9)

Below **Plan of the advance of the 42nd Division to the Michel Line. The blockhouses outside Charey are in square B36 and the St-Mihiel Cemetery is at B21.**
(USAMHI/Chambley/MFME MF 1/12)

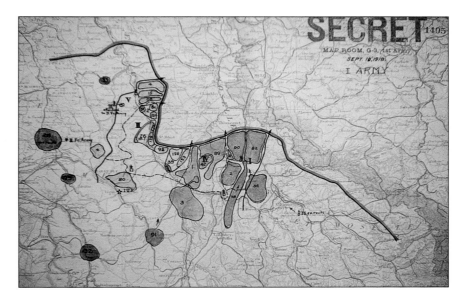

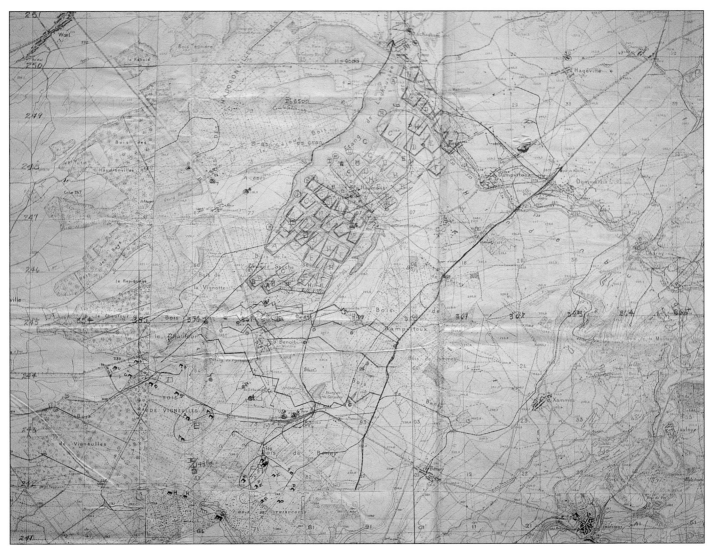

shot at. He wrote to his wife, 'Here I was nearvous [sic].' First he rolled off and took cover, then sought help from the infantry some 100 yards to the rear. When they appeared to lack the enthusiasm to do much about it, he chased after the tank, knocked with his stick on the rear door and, when it opened, told the obviously disappointed sergeant, who had been enjoying the drive, to take him back.

Forderhase, to his surprise, found the advance equally easy, though confused.

When German troops came out of their dugouts, they were clean and dry, we were muddy from head to foot from our long hike in the muddy trenches and across no-mansland. There was much confusion as the day's action continued. Troops of the divisions on our flanks intermingled with us... Only Company Commanders seemed to have any kind of map – a serious mistake – this in our first major combat operation... We continued to advance as we met no resistance. A halt was ordered as we reached the deep vale near Thiaucourt... we soon resumed the advance... [and] reached the second day's objective before 4pm of the first day.

They came to a German dugout where they found wine, brandy and 'some fancy-looking cigarettes that did not smell very good'. In the growing dark they went on until they came near a farm on the edge of a village. The exhausted men slumped to the ground while the buildings were reconnoitred, and by the time their lieutenant came back they were hard to rouse. They bedded down thankfully in the hayloft of the farm. They had reached Xammes in a single day.

The Germans were fleeing or surrendering as fast as they could. The attack had clearly been a surprise, for the advancing Americans found food still on the tables of the houses the enemy had occupied. Clothing and equipment was abandoned everywhere. By now the 304th's tanks had, except for a single vehicle, run out of fuel and Patton pushed on towards Pannes riding on the outside of the remaining Renault. Approaching the village of Beney, he noticed little chips of paint popping off the side of the tank and realised they were being

Left **Consolidating the line. A 37-mm anti-tank gun battery being set up near St-Benoit, 19 September. The weapon fired solid shot.** (USAMHI/ASC 22672) [5/17]

Below **A first-aid dressing station at Flirey.** (USAMHI/ASC 34891/WWI/ 30thDiv.55thFABde.Hansen, Harry) [10/11]

While the advance had been remarkable, the salient had not been closed. That night, part of the 26th Division marched along the Grande Tranchée de Calone from the north-west. Although it was entrenched in the war, it was originally the formal approach to a great château, bordered with rose bushes. The 26th struck along this ridgeway and had command of Vigneulles by 2am. The next morning the 1st Division pushed up from the south to join them by 10am. By that evening almost all of the objectives had been secured. Attention now turned to consolidating the American positions here and undertaking the second part of the operation – the mass transfer of the First Army to the new front between the Meuse and the Argonne.

Corporal Forderhase and his squad were in the Bois de Beney, north of the village of Beney, until 24 September.

The men were hungry and began to break out their rations. Some of them began to gather what dry twigs they could find in order to heat up a cup of coffee. I forbade my group to build a fire as I was sure the resulting smoke from it would draw the fire of German artillery. As soon as the smoke from these small fires was visible above the treetops the shelling began... When the first round came, I led my squad out of the area. An officer and I went back to the area after the shelling ceased to observe the effects. The destruction of the trees had to be seen to be believed. We also

Below **The American Monument crowns the Butte de Montsec.** (MFME Yp/Ar 5/21)

Bottom **From the Butte de Montsec the road runs to Richecourt and the German front line assaulted by the 42nd Division. The Forêt des Hauts de Mad is to the left in the distance.** (MFME Yp/Ar 5/23)

found a few pieces of equipment, and a helmet with about half a teacup of human brains in it. Too big a price to pay for a cup of hot coffee.

The establishment of the new front line was more than a routine matter. Captain F. M. Wood, in command of D Company, 353rd Infantry, 89th Division, had established contact with the Marines of the 2nd Division on his right at the end of the first day's fighting. The next day he saw

... the Marines charge up the slope at Mon Plaisir Farm and be literally blown into the air by direct artillery fire. They formed again and again, only to meet with the same results.

The farm was a fortified strongpoint of the Hindenburg Line, and was to remain in German hands until the Armistice was signed. Work now went ahead

Above **La Tranchée en Terre de St-Baussant, Site No. 5. The trenches taken by the 89th Division are preserved in the Forêt des Hauts de Mad.** (MFME Yp/Ar 5/29)

to create the new front line out of what had been the St-Mihiel Salient.

The army engineers laid down a plan of trench systems (on paper) which extended across and in rear of our positions. This new system to be the main line of resistance. This necessitated a great deal of work. The work of course must be done by the infantry. A great deal of digging and building of wire entanglements became the orders of the day and night. Work in the open must be confined to the night and even then the working parties were shelled and gassed.

Air cover was now all but non-existent, and covering fire from the artillery was lacking. The effort was now on another front. Probing raids were made to establish the exact positions of the enemy lines. In the early morning of 26 September a party under the command of Second Lieutenant Marshall P. Wilder of the

Forderhase and observed by the French, who remained sceptical about American staff abilities. In spite of these facts, the operation was vital to the Americans. They had captured 16,000 prisoners and 450 guns for the loss of only 7,000 killed, wounded and missing. Sooner or later their staff work had needed to be tried in battle. More importantly, the morale of the newly created, independent army of the United States needed to be raised to combat readiness by a clear victory. Without this experience they would not have been in condition to face the coming trial, the Battle of the Argonne.

Top **A statue of a young American officer stands in the St-Mihiel Cemetery.**
(MFME Yp/Ar 5/34 or 6/4)

Above **From the summit of the great hill above Les Éparges the plain of the Woevre stretches away towards Metz and the Moselle to the east.**
(MFME Yp/Ar 6/14)

Right **The village of Charey lies south-east of bunkers of the Michel Line surviving amongst the fields.**
(MFME Yp/Ar 6/6)

354th Infantry, 89th Division, climbed the ridge north of Xammes and, against some resistance, penetrated as far as the village of Charey, reconnoitring the layout of the German wire. Subsequent forays pinpointed the positions of the bunkers, the grey silhouettes of which still bulge above the wheatfields to this day.

The Americans were delighted with their success. It was, however, not quite such a marvel as it appeared. The order to vacate the salient and withdraw to the Michel Line had been given by Ludendorff on 8 September and was conveyed to the German units on the ground two days later. The German artillery was already moving back when the attack took place. The American First Army was therefore fighting a force that had to turn a planned withdrawal into a fighting retreat. Even in these favourable circumstances their progress was marked by the confusion reported by Corporal

IN AT THE FINAL LICKIN'

The shift in action from the eastern bank of the Meuse to the west, the other side of Verdun, was not supported by Douglas MacArthur, among others. He felt that a continued advance across the Woevre Plain towards Metz, the Moselle River and the heartland of Germany would bring the war to a swift end. By the same token, George Patton was to remember this as a lost opportunity 26 years later. Perhaps even more persuasive is the fact that the opportunity to cut the Germans' east-west railway between Metz and Verdun was not taken, although the lack of heavy tanks on this front made such action diffi-

Repington, the correspondent at the front for *The Times*, declared that it could not have been done better. The American First Army now held a front 94 miles long, from the western edge of the Argonne Forest to the new positions forward of St-Mihiel.

THE GERMAN LINES

The terrain the Americans faced was in part hilly, and in other parts even hillier. On the west the River Aisne divided the high, open country of Champagne from the near-mountains of the Argonne Forest, which run due north. The little River Aire flows north on the eastern

Only three roads, and minor ones at that, could be used by the 600,000 troops, 93,000 horses and all their support and equipment...

cult to contemplate. Lieutenant-General Hunter Liggett, commanding the American I Corps, took the view that such an operation would have been possible 'only on the supposition that our army was a well-oiled, fully co-ordinated machine, which it was not as yet.' Whatever their misgivings, however, the US forces threw themselves into the task of changing fronts.

The American front lay across the south of the Argonne Forest eastwards to the River Meuse, where it passed to the west of the heights above Verdun. Only three roads, and minor ones at that, could be used by the 600,000 troops, 93,000 horses and all their support and equipment which made the 60-mile journey from the St-Mihiel Salient. Colonel Marshall therefore designated one road for motor vehicles and the other two for men on foot and animals. To complicate matters, the French had to withdraw from the Argonne sector at the same time as the Americans moved in. Furthermore, the process could not begin until the St-Mihiel action was largely complete, on 14 September, and had to be finished in time for the new offensive to start on 26 September. There were delays, traffic jams and frustration, but a British observer, Colonel Charles

flank before turning west at St-Juvin and running past Grandpré to join the Aisne north of Binarville. East of the Aire the landscape is softer, lines of rolling hills running east to west, punctuated by thick woods and more prominent hilltops, the whole area sloping eventually to the valley of the Meuse with its broad flood plain. Beyond that river the land rises steeply to the Heights of the Meuse. In peacetime it is delightful, its little streams lively with trout and the air filled with a marvellous variety of birds. Even today the fields, farms and villages have an air of enviable tranquillity. As a theatre for mobile warfare, however, it was deeply unpromising.

The area had been the scene of continuous fighting in the first year of the war as the armies of the German Crown Prince Wilhelm, son and heir of Kaiser Wilhelm II, strove to break through the French lines. In the high woodland west of Varennes-en-Argonne, countless bloody encounters took place amongst trenches and blockhouses which can still to be seen today. The front line passed eastwards, south of Varennes, through the Height of Vauquois – once crowned with a healthy village. By September 1918 that village had been flattened, and where the houses once stood there gaped a hole

Above, left **German soldiers pose with a massive trench mortar. From a collection of captured pictures.** [10/19]

Above, right **Time out with a bottle of wine for German troops.** [10/22]

Below, left **A group of Germans with the widely deployed Minenwerfer, a 305-mm mortar.** [10/20]

Below, right **Building materials being transported by light railway for the construction of the Hindenburg Line.** [10/21]

(From a collection of captured pictures: USAMHI/WWI/33rdDiv.66th\Inf.124MGBn. Newman, Sergeant William W.)

60 feet deep. It was as though a giant knife-stroke had cut through the summit. Mining and counter-mining had blown Vauquois away entirely. During the months that followed, the French and Germans continued to torture one another from trenches 50 yards apart on the shattered lips of the crater. The front line then ran east to the north of Béthincourt, crossing the Meuse some ten miles north of Verdun.

The second-line position built up by the Germans in the relatively quiet years after 1915 was based on the hill of Montfaucon which, while appearing modest in height, dominates the country for miles around. In the west the Heights of the Argonne cover the flank here, as they do all the way north. In addition, through Apremont, Gesnes and on to Sivry on the Meuse, ran the Giselher Stellung. This carefully constructed

German defence used trenches, pillboxes and blockhouses to provide a supplementary line to the second position of resistance. Then came the third position, based on the hills at Romagne and running west to the north of Granpré, with a branch down to Exermont, and east to Brieulles and the Kriemhilde Stellung, the Hindenburg Line proper. A fourth position, unfinished but still a serious obstacle, was centred on the Barricourt Heights and ran westwards to Buzancy and to Dun-sur-Meuse in the east. There were also many switch lines, intermediate trenches, belts of barbed wire, fortified farms, pillboxes and support trenches between the major works. Nowhere had the Germans constructed a more formidable system of defences. Pershing, with his most experienced divisions in need of rest after the battle two weeks before, was forced to pit green troops against this barrier.

THE FIRST PHASE
On the left, facing the Argonne Forest, was Hunter Liggett's I Corps with the 77th, 28th and 35th Divisions. To the east, from Vauquois, was Lieutenant-General George H. Cameron's V Corps with the 91st, 37th and 79th Divisions, and alongside the French was Lieutenant-General Robert L. Bullard's III Corps with the 4th, 80th and 33rd Divisions. The barrage began half an hour before midnight on Wednesday, 25 September,

Below **Known as the Abri de Kronprinz, a complex of bunkers survives in the Bois de la Gruerie, south-east of Varennes-en-Argonne.**
(MFME Yp/Ar 3/35 or 4/1 or 4/2)

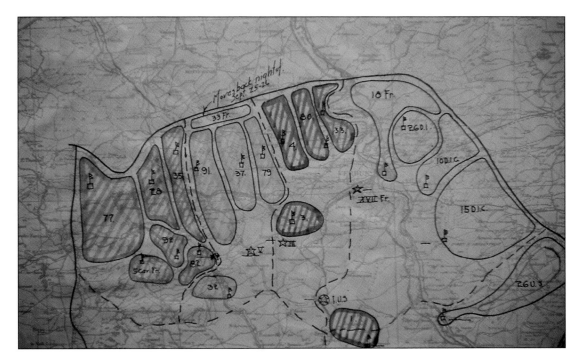

Left and right **The situation of the First Army on 24 September (left) and at 6pm, 25 September 1918 (right) on the Meuse-Argonne front, from the G-3 map. Yellow shading indicates French troops.** (USAMHI/MFME 7/27, 7/29 and 7/31)

Below, right **On the summit of the Butte de Vauquois the Germans were separated by a yawning man-made ravine from these old French trenches.** (MFME Yp/Ar 4/7)

when the long-range heavy artillery opened up on selected targets. The corps and divisional artillery joined in the barrage at 2.30am on the 26th. The new boys of the untested divisions were overwhelmed by the astounding noise, and amazed at the brightness that illuminated the night.

At 5.30am the 59 operational tanks of 354th Battalion, I Tank Brigade, US Tank Corps moved off with the 35th Division to join 137th and 138th Infantry Regiments in the assault to the west of Vauquois, towards Cheppy. The battalion report relates that there was very dense fog and that progress was slow, although resistance was light. They had reached a hill just south of Cheppy (L54, page 76) by 9.15am when, as the fog lifted, the German guns began to shell them. George Patton, not content to remain at headquarters, had taken command of I Brigade in the field and ordered the 354th to attack. Their way was blocked by two disabled French Schneider tanks, but the nimble Renaults set off left and right of the hill, coming under fire from artillery near Varennes to their rear. That soon ceased, doubtless silenced by the 28th Division on their left. Part of the 354th and the 137th Infantry tackled the trenches south and west of Cheppy, while the rest of the tank battalion went to the aid of the 138th Infantry. The village was taken. Captain Ranulf Compton of the 354th writes in his report:

The infantry losses had been very heavy up to this time, both from shellfire and machine-guns. The machine-gun fire was silenced, but the shellfire continued. There was no counter-artillery fire apparently, and the Boche planes flew over con-

stantly until the middle of the afternoon, observing and directing artillery fire. Lieut.-Colonel Patton had been wounded at about the time the 354th was ordered into the attack.

Patton's account was somewhat more colourful. The tanks were moved forward over the enemy trench in front of Cheppy, courtesy of some hurried digging by

Above **The shell-shattered hill of Montfaucon, crowned with the ruins of the monastery, like broken teeth.** (USAMHI/ 141906-311.3-278.3) [6/21]

Right **From the newly won height of Montfaucon French and American observers view the next objective.** (USAMHI/ASC 24443) [6/24]

a crew of infantrymen – Patton had bullied them into the work – and by hitching one tank to another to heave it over the obstacle. On foot, Patton then led the re-formed infantry forward until enemy fire pinned them down. Losing patience with grovelling in the mud, he said to himself, 'It is time for another Patton to die,' and with that he called for a further advance, during which he was hit. The bullet went in through his groin and exited through a buttock. His orderly, Private Joseph Angelo, fixed a field dressing and relayed Patton's orders until the position was taken. More than a month later he was still in hospital with a badly infected wound, but he recovered sufficiently to make an unauthorised exit in time to celebrate the Armistice.

To the right of the 35th, the 91st Division pushed briskly forward through Cheppy Woods virtually unopposed. As the fog lifted they, too, came under fire from the Butte de Vauquois on the left, both from artillery and from the numerous machine-gun nests in the woods. As the divisional history points out, these machine-gun emplacements were positioned to fire to the flank, covering the approaches to the neighbouring

gun, or gaps in the barbed wire. The source of flanking fire is always hard to locate, and each nest has to be taken out by tanks or artillery before further advance is possible. A frontal attack is suicide, and an infantry flanking movement almost as dangerous. The rest of the division hurried across the open ground and into the cover of Cheppy Woods. On the northern side of the woods they were held up for a while at La Neuve Grange Farm (L72), but by noon they had made it to the village of Véry (L55). They dug in north of the village for the night while, in their rear, the engineers laboured to rebuild roads so that supplies could move forward into Cheppy Woods. They had advanced five miles that day. On the extreme right the 80th and 33rd Divisions had made a similar advance to establish a blocking line along the Meuse. On the extreme left the 77th had crossed the Varennes-Le Four de Paris road but stumbled at the salient made by the continued resistance of the bunkers around the Abri de Kronprinz (the concrete strongholds are still standing today). The 28th Division found the going harder in the valley of the Aire, enduring flanking fire from the forest on their left.

Below **In the remains of the Argonne Forest, near Le Four de Paris, the 77th Division pause before the attack of 26 September.** (National Archives/ASC 22342)

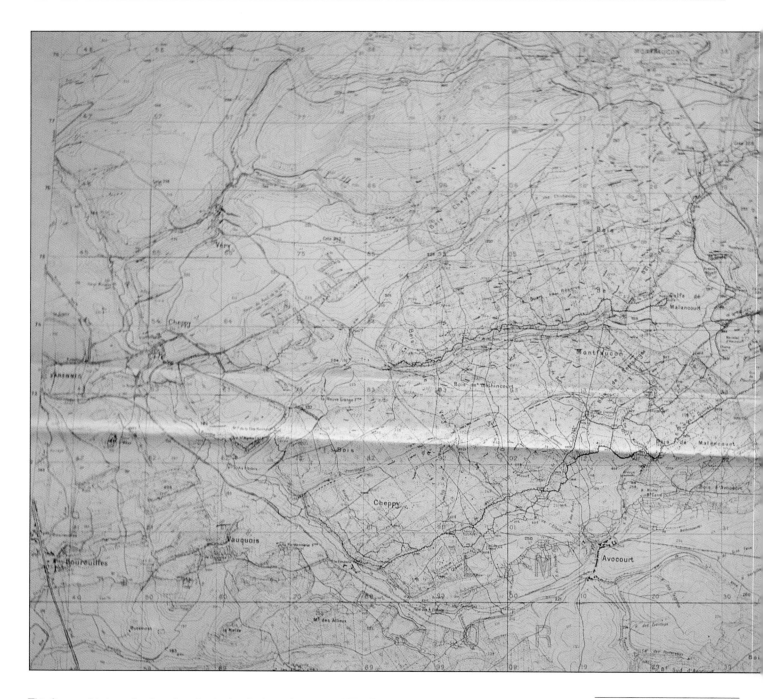

This fire would slow all units advancing in the shadow of the forest in the coming weeks. It was the 79th Division that had the toughest time as they made for the commanding height of Montfaucon. From this observation point the German artillery was directed on to pre-registered targets directly in the path of the Americans. The results were fearful. As a consequence the 4th Division on their right were held up, allowing the Germans to reinforce Nantillois and the Brieulles Woods.

In fact Colonel Billy Mitchell's airmen were there, contrary to the complaints of the troops on the ground. The First Pursuit Group flew low-level missions, shooting down four balloons and eight aircraft, while the Second operated at a higher altitude, accounting for seven German machines. Mitchell himself flew over the battlefield and saw a severe traffic jam near Avocourt. He ordered First Day Bombardment Group to carry out a diversionary attack on Dun-sur-Meuse to draw the Germans away and to dislocate their supply lines. Despite all these efforts, however, air support was comparatively slender, in the absence of the French and British reinforcement enjoyed at St-Mihiel.

Above **Map of the sector attacked by V Corps on 26 September, with German trenches (blue) and the American front line (red) updated to 12 August 1918.**
(USAMHI/MFME MF 1/14)

General Max von Gallwitz, commander of the Group comprising the German Third and Fifth Armies, was at first worried that the attack was a feint to cover a renewed onslaught in the Woevre. However, he swiftly appreciated that this thrust was the Americans' prime effort and transferred fresh troops to the sectors under attack. He was confident his series of defence lines could hold against such inexperienced troops. The days that followed appeared to justify his optimism.

The first line of the German defence had fallen easily, but the second, through Montfaucon, took another three days to conquer. American units flanked the pinnacle of Montfaucon on both sides before a costly assault reduced it on 27 September. The attackers thus gained a viewpoint from which they could see the positions of the Kriemhild Line. In the Argonne Forest the 77th Division clawed forward, often disorientated and sometimes ambushed in the thick woodlands. Where, in more open territory, swifter progress might have been expected, co-operation between tanks and infantry was lacking, exposing both to higher casualties than they would have incurred operating in concert. On 28

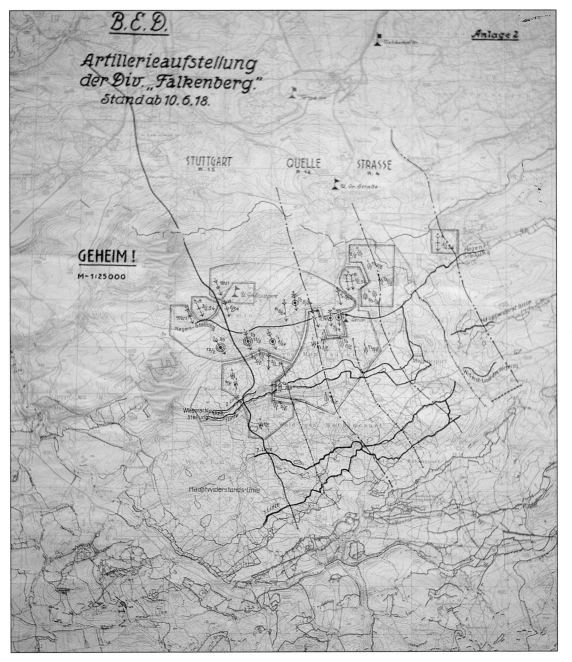

Right **German artillery map for the sector south of Montfaucon drawn up on 10 June 1918.** (USAMHI/MFME MF 1/17)

September, Ranulf Compton reports, the western group of 354th Battalion's tanks advanced from Montblainville and entered Apremont at noon. They were unaccompanied by infantry and, despite clearing the Germans out, were not the appropriate force to hold the town. The men of the 28th Division, the Keystone Division from Pennsylvania, had taken Varennes (where their monument now stands) the day before, but now found themselves under the German guns on Le Chêne Tondu, the high bluffs overlooking Apremont. The 354th was summoned to help, but it was not until evening that they obtained the support of a small infantry unit to secure the town they had reached at midday.

The eastern group of the tank battalion got as far as Exermont on 29 September, but once again outran the infantry, the much-weakened 35th Division, and had to withdraw. The town would not be taken until 4 October. Artillery support was also poorly co-ordinated, depending too much on firing blind, although a notable exception was an action in support of the 35th

Above **The 112th Engineers, 37th Division, labour to repair the roads near Montfaucon.** (USAMHI/ASC 42278/WWI/37thDiv. Dennis, Dallas D.) [10/26]

'It was a great sight... everything clockwork, setting fuses, cutting fuses, slapping shells into breeches and jerking lanyards...'

Division. On 30 September a balloon observer reported to that division's 110th Field Signal Battalion that the Germans were gathering to counter-attack a forward infantry unit. There were no telephone lines to the artillery, so Paul Shaffer had to run with the message to D Battery, 149th Field Artillery, and deliver the message to its commander, Captain Harry S. Truman – later to be President of the United States from 1945-53. Shaffer later recounts:

... When he read my message he started runnin' and cussin' all at the same time, shouting for the guns to turn north-west. He ran about a hundred yards to a little knoll, and what he saw didn't need binoculars. I never heard a man cuss so well or so intelligently, and I'd shoed a million mules. He was shouting back ranges and giving bearings. The battery didn't say a word. They must have figured the cap'n could do the cussin' for the whole outfit. It was a great sight... everything clockwork, setting fuses, cutting fuses, slapping shells into breeches and jerking lanyards [to fire the guns]...

Swept up in the spirit of the moment, Shaffer followed Truman up the little hill where, across the fields in front of them, they saw groups of Germans on the edge of a wood, creeping forward with weapons at the ready. Truman yelled fresh orders, and the next salvo scattered

dismembered enemy soldiers in all directions. The danger was averted. In 1948 that captain was running for President. Shaffer gave him his vote.

Behind the front line there were more difficulties for the Americans. The few narrow roads that wound north into the area crossed terrain devastated by shell-fire, which had been no man's land for nearly four years. The engineers strove to make new roads, but their work was undone as fast as it was completed, either by enemy fire or by attempts to move heavy guns and tanks forward. Although the first day of the offensive had been dry, rain had been falling ever since and the guns had to be moved forward with the help of infantrymen heaving on ropes. Pershing, disappointed with progress, went to visit his corps commanders; he makes no mention in his memoirs of the fact that it took him 90 minutes to travel two and a half miles when doing so. On Sunday, 29 September, the French Prime Minister, Clemenceau, attempted to visit Montfaucon. The chaos on the road prevented him reaching his destination.

It was clear that the divisions which had gone into the attack only three days earlier were at the end of their endurance. The 35th had been cut to ribbons and

Fourth Army, which was held up at Somme-Py.'
Pershing's great stride forward had come to a halt.

THE FRENCH FLANK

The attack of 26 September involved the French as
well. To the west of the Argonne Forest the French
161st Division was also striking north and with them
three regiments of the American 93rd Division (a unit
which was never to operate as a division). These were
the 369th, 371st and 372nd Infantry, in the parlance of
that time, negro regiments. Mainly officered by white
soldiers, they had trained with the French, wore mainly
French uniforms and fought with French equipment.
The abilities of black soldiers in this war are discussed
in depth in other books. It is enough to say that the use
made of them in 1918 scarcely allowed them to do
themselves justice. The French, however, did not share
their American ally's doubts about these men, and their
confidence was well rewarded.

On 26 September, the 369th was in support of the
attack to the west of Cernay-en-Dormois, but the regiment was soon brought forward to help overcome the
resistance of the Germans at Rouvroy-Ripont on the
River Dormoise. They took the town and, the next day,
took Fontaine-en-Dormois and gained a hold on the
slopes of Bellevue Signal Ridge to the north. On 28
September the 371st and 372nd came into the line on
the 369th's right, to the other side of the French unit
alongside them, and the drive continued. Ardeuil on the
left and Séchault on the right fell the next day. The black
soldiers' courage was high but their casualties were

had lost all coherence. The 1st Division were sent to
relieve them, while the 82nd were on their way to give
the battered 28th a break. In the centre the 3rd and the
32nd assumed the ground of the 91st, 37th and 79th
Divisions. 'It was a matter of keen regret,' Pershing was
to write, 'that the veteran 2nd Division was not on hand
at this time, but at Marshal Foch's earnest request it had
been sent to General Gouraud to assist the French

Below **American soldiers, 1918. Left, a captain wearing an overcoat with an Austrian knot on the cuff indicating rank. Right, a regimental supply sergeant of the 371st Infantry, 161st French Division, holding a French Berthier M1916 rifle. The canister holds his French gas mask and he wears a French standard issue Adrian helmet.**
(Osprey, MAA 230 *US Army 1890-1920*)
(*Jeffrey Burn*)

heavy. The three regiments had 2,246 killed, wounded and missing by the time the last of them, the 372nd, was relieved on 7 October. By then they had won the admiration of one of the toughest of the French divisions, the 2nd Moroccan, which was fighting on their left.

THE HINDENBURG LINE

If the close of September was a time of failure and reassessment in the Argonne, it was a time of victory to the west. While the Americans hit the Germans at St-Mihiel and in the Argonne, the British struck at Arras and Cambrai to the north, and in Flanders further north. By late September the British were once more face to face with the Hindenburg Line, here called the Siegfried Line, based on the St-Quentin Canal which ran

north from that town towards Cambrai. The principal fortification was on the eastern bank, but the canal runs through a tunnel from Riqueval northwards, passing beneath Bellicourt and Bony, to emerge at Le Catelet. The hill above the tunnel was protected by entrenchments, bunkers and barbed wire of amazing complexity. Monash's Australian Corps was by now extremely tired, having taken part in every British action since the previous April. As a result, and to the Australian's delight, the American 27th and 30th Divisions reinforced the British for this operation.

Private J. Walter Strauss, with the 102nd Engineers, 27th Division, described the Siegfried Line.

These defenses consisted generally of three strong lines of trenches, protected by an extraordinary mass of wire... There were 25 barges in the main tunnel and these were used by the Germans as billets for reserve troops... Along the easterly side of the tunnel there had been sunk through the ground above a number of approaches to the tunnel towpath... In similar manner passageways had been excavated from the westerly side of the canal to the main line of resistance constructed in the ground above and a short distance westerly of the line of the tunnel. No bombardment, no matter how severe, could affect reserve troops... [The] trenches had been perfected with dugouts, concrete machine-gun and mortar emplacements and underground shelters. They were protected by belt after belt of barbed wire entanglements...

led an attack against the Knoll, taking two machine-gun posts and then pushing forward over four lines of trenches. He died in the counter-attack that followed. Sergeant Reidar Waaler risked his life saving men from a burning British tank. But the heroism of individuals was not enough. By the next morning it had become evident that the 106th had failed in its attack and had taken heavy losses, 1,540 casualties in all. It was also probable that many men were isolated in no man's land, directly in the path of a further offensive. To their right the 30th Division had also suffered, though not on the same scale.

On the morning of 29 September they attacked again. Fearful of killing their own men, they put their barrage 1,000 yards ahead of the advancing troops and chased to catch up. With the American 301st Heavy Tank Battalion in British Mark V tanks in support, the 27th and 30th Divisions pushed forward through thick fog. Once again they were met with lethal machine-gun

Above **The 33rd and 80th Divisions were on the eastern flank. From the hills above Sivry-sur-Meuse the terrain taken by the 80th is overlooked by Montfaucon, seen on the horizon with the pinnacle of the American Monument rising from it.** (MFME Yp/Ar 5/13)

What was more, these obstacles were sited so as to channel attackers into the path of fixed-aim machine-guns. At the same time, field guns were dug in and concealed to shell tanks which were similarly beguiled into the line of fire.

The outposts of the Siegfried Line ran from north to south just east of the villages of Lempire, Hargicourt and Villeret. For the assault, the northern sector, Lempire-Hargicourt, was assigned to the 27th Division while the 30th took over the southern half. At 5.30am on 27 September the 106th Infantry, 27th Division, supported by 12 tanks of the British 4th Battalion, Tank Corps, moved to take strongpoints, the Knoll north-west of Bony, Guillemont Farm west of the village and Quennemont Farm to the south-west. Smoke shells added to the obscurity of that foggy morning. The regiment was seriously short of officers and of experienced non-commissioned officers, so as the casualties among their commanders mounted, confusion set in. Acts of bravery were numerous. Lieutenant William B. Turner

Below **Corporal Freddie Stowers, 371st Infantry, 93rd Division, lies in the American Meuse-Argonne Cemetery. He was awarded the Congressional Medal of Honor.** (MFME 4/35)

Bottom **A German observation post in the ruins of the monastery at Montfaucon.** (MFME Yp/Ar 4/18)

and artillery fire. Their courage was beyond doubt, but skill was lacking. Again their casualties were heavy and their progress slow, while the tanks fell victim to a new sophistication in the way the German field guns were deployed. Of 141 tanks engaged, 75 were hit, some of them destroyed while crossing an old British minefield.

Private Strauss reports that his F Company, 102nd Engineers, was used as a combat unit that day, moving towards a machine-gun post near Guillemont Farm.

...As we were advancing, a sudden shower of shells hit us and I dove into a shell hole. As I did so, I felt a thud in my side from a machine-gun the Germans had at the knoll. I crawled back into a trench for better protection and found a German machine-gun bullet had gone through a first-aid packet on the right side of my pack, then on into my Bible (New Testament) and lodged there. A quarter of an inch to the right would have punctured my lung and I would have

Left **The black soldiers of what was intended to be the 93rd Division served with the French and used French equipment.** (USAMHI/WWI/VICorps. Sweeney, Major William R.) [8/21]

Right **Aerial photograph, 17 September 1918, of the terrain at Bony, an objective of the US 27th Division. The complex of German trenches can be seen on either side of the road running left to right through the village.** (TM 5086/D4)

Below, left **American troops prepare to move to the attack with British Mark V tanks carrying cribs, wooden cylinders for dropping into trenches or shell-holes that would otherwise prevent progress.** (TM 421/F5)

'Rested. Bath in p.m. at Templeux la Fosse. Clean underwear. Wow!'

died quickly. This was the Bible given to me by our Camp Mother, Mrs Ella Hight, back in May (9th) 1918 at Belvoir, Virginia...We kept pushing the Germans back and they kept shelling us with gas shells, phosgene and mustard gas.

Private Edward L. North, 102nd Field Signal Battalion, 27th Division, had little time to write home

that morning. He stuffed the letter he had just received from his brother (Charles, who was serving with 302nd Field Signal Battalion) into an envelope and scrawled a note: 'Going out for a long hike this a.m. for the day. Rec'd letter from Charlie last night. Will enclose it as he requested. Love to all, Edward.' A long hike it was.

Pushing towards Bellicourt, the 30th Division's progress was at first encouraging. However, they were slowed by the elaborate system of tunnels which allowed the Germans to emerge in their rear once the attackers had passed over. Private Willard M. Newton of the 105th Engineers, 30th Division, was 18 years old. His company was in a trench with the 117th Infantry before the attack started.

We are all full of cheer and anxiously waiting for the shelling to start. The infantrymen are as full of cheer as we. They are anxious to get a whack at Fritz. When asked by the doughboys what we are going to do, we say 'build and repair roads', not really knowing what we would do before the day is over... At last we are at the beginning of a real battle between Prussianism and Democracy!

Scores of dead Americans, Australians and Germans can be seen lying here and there, some covered with raincoats and overcoats and others lying just as they fell. Walking wounded

are going back in twos and threes, while those unable to walk are being carried off of the field as rapidly as possible under the circumstances. Men with arms shot off, with slight shrapnel wounds and gassed victims are being helped to the rear by German prisoners and by other men similarly wounded... Packs, rifles, cartridge belts, wrecked ammunition wagons, hand grenades, and ammunition of every size and kind are scattered everywhere in great quantities.

Newton spent the better part of the day in shell holes and captured bunkers, waiting for orders. At about 3pm he was detailed with seven others to carry two wounded men to the rear. It was sunset before they got back. One of the men had died on the way and all of the carriers were badly gassed.

The Australians formed the second wave of attack. They intended to pass through the positions the Americans had taken and go forward from there. But both the Australian 3rd Division, behind the American 27th, and the 5th Division which was moving up to the 30th, found their allies still struggling against their early objectives. The Americans refused the relief. Side by side the two nations fought on, doggedly reducing the German strongpoints until, as darkness fell, the line was finally broken. The victory had been expensively bought. The 27th had 3,500 men killed, wounded and missing and their Australian friends of the 3rd Division suffered 1,000 casualties. The 30th took 1,881 casualties and, by 2 October the Australian 5th had lost 1,500 officers and men. On 3 October Strauss wrote: 'Rested. Bath in p.m. at Templeux la Fosse. Clean underwear. Wow!'

The attack as a whole on 29 September enjoyed considerable success, though not in the massively fortified sector above the tunnel. Further south, at Riqueval Bridge over the St-Quentin Canal and at Bellenglise, the

Map of the Siegfried Line from Bellicourt to Riqueval Bridge, with German trenches in blue, updated to 19 September 1918. The blue crayon line is the front line immediately prior to the attack of 29 September and was marked by the map's user, A. J. Gurr of the British 6th Tank Battalion. The American 30th Division faced the German fortifications at Bellicourt while the attempt to cross the canal at the bridge between Pike Copse and Blacktown, which was not thought to have much chance of success, was made by the 1/6th North Staffordshire Regiment. (TM Accn 442.6/8[3])

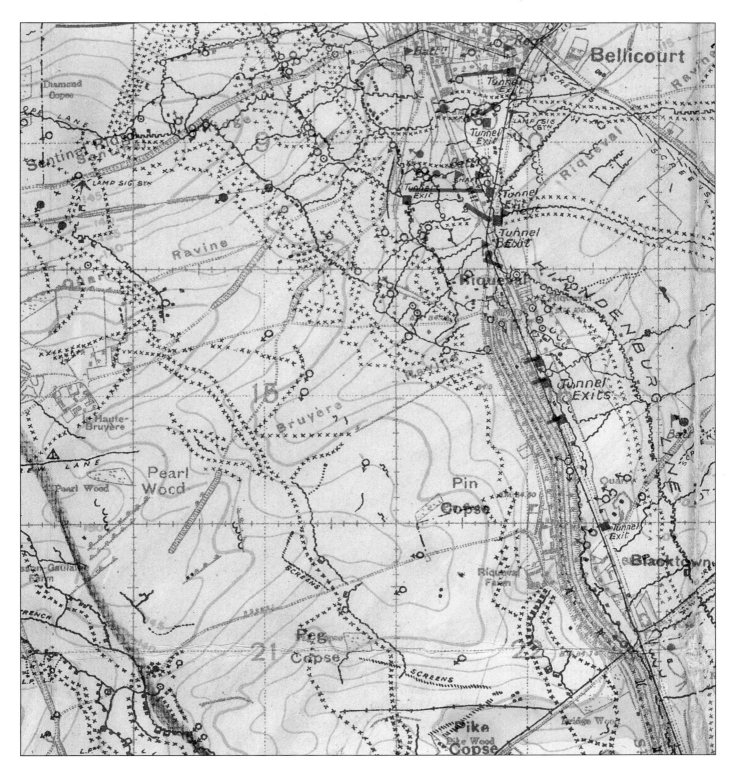

Left **Escorted by, and carrying one of, the men of the 27th Division, German prisoners help with the wounded at Ronssoy, 27 September 1918.**
(USAMHI/ASC 28198) [6/34]

Below **Salvation Army workers provide doughnuts at Varennes, 12 October 1918.**
(USAMHI/ASC 29503) [9/18]

Above **A German machine-gun emplacement on the Siegfried Line, photographed on 3 October.** (USAMHI/ASC 25977) [7/6]

Souain, a town of the dead, a shattered skeleton of a place, with shells breaking over it. Beyond and northward was Somme-Py, nearly blotted out by years of war. From there to the horizon, east and west and north and south, was all a stricken land. The rich topsoil that formerly made the Champagne one of the fat provinces of France was gone, blown away and buried under by four years of incessant shellfire.

With a map laid out on the ground, the situation was described to the platoon leaders and non-commissioned officers.

The Frogs have driven the Boche a kilometre and a half north of Somme-Py. You see it here – the town you watched them shell this morning. They have gotten into the Prussian trench – this blue line with the wire in front of it. It's just a fire trench, mostly shellholes linked up. Behind it, quite close, is the Essen trench, which is evidently a humdinger! Concrete pillboxes and deep dugouts and all that sort of thing – regular fort. The Frogs say it can't be taken from the front – they've tried. We're goin' to take it. On the other side of that is the Elbe trench, and a little to the left the Essen Hook, and in the centre the Bois de Vipre – same kind o' stuff, they say. We're to take them... Next, away up in this corner of the map, is the Blanc Mont place. Whoever is left when we get that far will take that, too.

In the event, the Marines found the Essen Trench in the process of being evacuated by the Germans as the Americans arrived in the fire trench, and thankfully occupied it themselves on 2 October. The 5th Marines were on the left of the line with the 6th to their right, and beyond them the 9th and then the 23rd Infantry. The Marines were to attack the left flank of the Blanc Mont Ridge while the infantry were to take the right, the centre being held by reserves. In front of the infantry were the French, holding what were to be the jump-off trenches for the next day, but their 170th Division were driven out by the Germans, relieved by the French 167th, and fell back without communicating with their allies.

At dawn on 3 October, supported by artillery and tanks, the 2nd Division began its task. The 5th Marines outflanked and took the Essen Hook, while the 6th made for the ridge through a hail of artillery and machine-gun fire. Private Francis of the 5th Marines later recalled:

It was cold and we were wearing overcoats. I usually went over the top with a loaf of bread inside my blouse... I was always eating on it, not especially as I wanted it but because it took my mind off the fighting sometimes... We broke the German lines and gained our objective the first day.

By noon the Marines were on the ridge. On the right the infantry also made spectacular progress. By 8.40am they were attacking Médéah Farm on the

men of the British 46th (North Midland) Division crossed the canal in spirited actions which took them to the east bank by 9am. The Germans had relied too much on the waterway itself. It had fallen to a swift attack in the foggy morning at the bridge, and to the ingenuity of the engineers in devising rafts and boats to cross the canal to the south. Whether this operation would have been completed with so little loss and so much gain had the Americans not been subjecting the Germans to ferocious pressure at Bony and Bellicourt is a question worth considering.

BLANC MONT

The French Fourth Army was fighting northwards to the west of the American First Army in the Argonne, hauling themselves forward over the often fiercely contested ground of Champagne. From the height of the Ferme de Navarin, north of Suippes, the land slopes gently down to the valley in which lies Somme-Py (Sommepy-Tahure on modern maps) and just as gently rises again. The road runs through broad, neatly cultivated fields to the wooded ridge of Blanc Mont. The American 2nd Division came here on 1 October. That far ridge was held by the Germans, dominating the land as far as Reims to the west and the Argonne Forest to the east, and nothing the French had tried would remove them.

Lieutenant John W. Thomason, Jr, B Company, 5th Marines, described the scene in his book.

North from the edge of the pines the battalion looked out on desolation where once the grassy, rolling slopes of the Champagne stretched away like a great white sea that has been dead and accursed through all time. Near at hand was

Mazagran road just beyond the ridge, but the French on their right had not kept up. Nor had they kept up on the Marines' left. As evening fell the troops in both wings of the 2nd Division's front were holding salients, exposed on three sides to enemy fire. The next day, leaving men to cover the outside flanks, the Marines fought their way up Blanc Mont and succeeded in joining across the top of the ridge, where the monument to them now stands. Private Francis said:

...The French did not keep up with us, so that we were being fired upon from the front, each side and nearly from the rear. We were afraid that the Germans were going to close in together in the rear and cut us off from our lines. We fought desperately to keep the Germans from carrying out their plans. We were on a prairie with machine-gun bullets hitting alround. They were hitting only inches from me on each side, and knocking dirt in my face. It seemed impossible for anyone to live through it... Later in the afternoon we took a German trench... That evening we stayed in a ravine and kept watch all night... About two o'clock in the morning someone was coming in, and we thought sure the Germans were attacking but it proved to be the French Chasseurs and they were surely welcomed.

The 2nd Division was holding a front about 500 yards wide, projecting one and a half miles into German lines. They stayed there through 5 October to allow the French to come up all along the line. It was a long day, 25 hours to be exact, for the clocks were changed from summer time to winter time. The next day the men of the 2nd were off again, Francis among them:

In the morning we started our drive again. We had only gone a little distance when we ran into the worst thing to face in the War – a three-inch gun firing point-blank at us, and just above 500 yards in front of us was a German 77...

Above **The American Memorial at Bellicourt overlooks the terrain over which the 27th and 30th Divisions fought to break the Siegfried Line.** (MFME Hist/Somme 5/10)

Left **The memorial at the Ferme de Navarin honours the French, American, Russian and other nationalities who fought against the invader.** (MFME Yp/Ar 3/27)

Below **From the French memorial at the Ferme de Navarin, south of Sommepy, the distant woods of Blanc Mont (left) stand on the horizon, dominated by the American monument.** (MFME Yp/Ar 3/24 or 3/25)

Opposite **The St-Quentin Canal runs between high banks south of the tunnel mouth.** (MFME Hist/Somme 5/7)

By the Armistice some 53,000 men – more than those killed in action – were to die of influenza.

It was awful, only a few yards in front men were blown to little bits, trees were knocked down; it didn't last long but it was surely terrible when it did.

By the night of 8 October 71 Infantry Brigade, 36th Division, had come up to relieve them and was digging in at the place where the 5th Marines had fought their way forward, St Étienne-à-Arnes, the German fourth line of resistance. Having lost the ridge and in the face of the continuing aggression of the 2nd Division and their French comrades, the Germans had fallen back. The 2nd had taken 4,973 casualties in this battle, 726 killed, 3,662 wounded and 585 missing. They now needed rest, but some of them did not get it. Their 15th Field Artillery and Second Lieutenant John D. Clark stayed with the 36th, the Lone Star Division, all the way to the Aisne. They reached the river on 27 October, having baffled the enemy, who were tapping their communication lines, by sending messages spoken in Choctaw. Clark noted a detail before leaving for the Argonne.

Along the road yesterday I saw a keen display of humor. Stuck on one of the posts of a barbed-wire prison pen was a placard reading 'Paris' advertising to the Boche confined there that at last they had reached their goal.

THE PAUSE IN THE ARGONNE

At the start of October General Pershing was under increasing pressure to make markedly better progress on the Meuse-Argonne front. Elsewhere all was advance; only here was the German line holding. Marshal Foch even went so far as to write an order transferring the American forces astride the Argonne Forest to French command. Pershing rejected it angrily. In any case, by 4 October he had regrouped, putting more experienced divisions into the line, and was ready to attack once again. The four-day pause had been used to advantage by the Germans as well. They had brought fresh troops to the Kriemhild Line and were ready for the onslaught. Pershing's best units were, however, composed of replacement troops to a significant extent and

Right **Men of the 308th Infantry, 77th Division, in a captured German trench, 26 September.** (National Archives/ASC 22343)

he had suffered losses from other causes as well. The great 'Spanish' influenza epidemic which had started that year reduced his force by 16,000 men during the first week of the month. By 1 November the sick in the AEF would total 306,719 with 19,429 deaths, and by the Armistice some 53,000 men – more than those killed in action – were to die of influenza.

To add to his difficulties, Pershing was desperately short of transport. He begged horses from the French, but they were themselves seriously lacking in animals. To bring more from America was only possible if other, vital supplies were left at home. It was Pershing's lowest time during the war, but, to the admiration of George Marshall, he soldiered on. The US Secretary of War, Newton D. Baker, supported him stoutly, persuading the British to release more shipping. But the immediate problem could not wait – the Kriemhild Line.

THE LOST BATTALION

On 4 October the assault began again. In the forest the 77th Division floundered forward through the thick scrub and shattered trees. Fragmented units pushed on, losing touch with their fellows. From the Bois d'Apremont, west of the village of that name, a little stream runs down a gully to Charlevaux. Here a mixed detachment of the 1st and 2nd Battalions, 308th Infantry, 77th Division, some 650 men under Major Charles W. Whittlesey, had already been pinned down for two days. In the confusion of the woods they had pushed forward of their regiment and were crouched at the foot of a steep slope. Higher up the Germans poured gunfire on them and rolled grenades amongst them. So steep was the hill that, fortunately, neither artillery nor mortar fire could be brought to bear on them. There the Americans held on as best they could, ammunition and rations dwindling. Repeated attempts to drop supplies to them from the air failed, since their white identification panels could not be seen through the thick forest. Attacks to relieve them also failed. On 7 October the Germans sent an American prisoner to them with a note inviting surrender. The response was defiance. Later that day the 77th Division finally pushed the line forward far enough to release them from their enclave. There were 195 men left unwounded.

THE KRIEMHILD LINE

In the Aire Valley the tattered remains of the 35th Division were replaced with Pershing's favourites, the 1st. On the way to the front to fight, Private Herbert L. McHenry, Machine-Gun Company, 16th Infantry, saw an impressive display of French determination, bravery and commitment.

Scattered about that field were badly crippled French soldiers. Some had a leg off, some an arm gone, others were

shot up in other ways, but they were manning machine-guns and anti-aircraft guns, protecting us from the Germans as they attacked from the air. From those old crippled soldiers, as they heroically continued to do duty, we knew that all France was on the battleline and bled white.

Earl D. Seaton, 16th Infantry, was also there:

As we moved up colored troops were repairing roads some places, sort of plank, but instead of planks, logs were used. I forget what they said but they did not expect to see any of us come back...We marched by a large pile of French bread, the loaves with holes in the center for your arm... I held up five fingers... we picked up five loaves. The pile was at least nine feet high. We bedded down the first night near Cheppy... Soon after dark the Germans started up the valley with battery fire.

The roads were clogged with supply wagons moving forward and ambulances moving back. German artillery harassment was constant.

Left **Map of the Argonne Forest with German trenches (as known) in blue and French/American trenches in red, updated to 19 September 1918. The Abri de Kronprinz is at square L01 and Le Four de Paris at U68. From Apremont, P98 in the north, the road runs west to Charlevaux Mill, P46 and Binarville, P35. It was in the gully to the south of that road, at P46-56, that the Lost Battalion was pinned down.** (USAMHI/MFME MF1/3)

Left **Above the ravine in which they were trapped stands a memorial stone to the men of the Lost Battalion.** (MFME Yp/Ar 4/26)

Below **The creek on which the Lost Battalion fought runs from the east into the lake at Charlevaux.** (MFME Yp/Ar 4/31)

The attack at 5am on 4 October was without pre-liminary bombardment, but it nevertheless came as no surprise to the Germans. Once more the co-ordination of the American effort was poor. Seaton was following the attack with a squad to establish telephone communication and ran into shellfire.

We found ourselves in the front line where shelling was heavy and the land was level. A shell hit on our right. A soldier had both feet blown off. The man behind him had his head mashed. I tied bandages around his stumps and stuck his rifle up by the bayonet, helmet on top, to mark for the first-aid crew. To the right a man fell on an exploding shell. It lifted his body into the air. We continued on.

Through a little wood, over a road, they struggled forward. A German gun emplacement was overrun. The squads became mixed up, and ad-hoc commanders took over mixed groups to go forward once more. They stopped just short of Fléville, having taken the Exermont valley in this haphazard fashion. Seaton turned to domestic tasks.

We stopped in an orchard. There was a supply dump here and on the side of the hill I used long shovel handles to create a sort of shelter... A sniper was shooting at me and I could hear the bullets go through the brush. In my shelter. I rigged up to cook cabbage and corned beef. I used carbide – no smoke [mixed with water, carbide gives off acetylene gas].

On 7 October the 82nd Division came through the 1st and attacked westwards, into the forested hills overlooking Cornay. This unexpected manoeuvre took the Germans by surprise and eased the pressure on the 28th and 77th, allowing the latter to retrieve their 'lost battalion'. In the broken woodlands Acting Corporal Alvin C. York had an opportunity to use his Tennessee woodsman's skills. His patrol had succeeded in surprising and capturing a group of 15 or so Germans when they came under fire. They took cover and, with his comrades guarding the captives, York steadily returned fire. A file of Germans moved to attack York, who – just as he would have dealt with a line of wild turkeys – picked off the last man first, then the second to last and so on until all six lay dead. When York came in from patrol he brought back three wounded buddies and 132 prisoners, and left 15 Germans dead in the woods.

The 16th Infantry then had the task of taking Hill 272, the last height before the Kriemhild Line itself. On the morning of 9 October, McHenry reports:

...The whole terrain was draped by a heavy fog. That fog was so heavy that it seemed to be black. We had intended to take up a position as would enable us to shoot overhead, over our infantry as it charged Hill 272, but owing to that fog we could not see to shoot anywhere.

The 16th stormed the hill and, in spite of their losses, took it. The valley before them was bounded on the

north by the principal German system of defence. The 1st Division had increased the Argonne advance to a total of ten miles since the start of the offensive, but they, too, were exhausted and the 42nd Division took over from them.

There is no letter to his mother from Major Raymond B. Austin, 6th Field Artillery, dated after 29 September. The last letter on the file, 20 April 1923, is addressed to Mr C. B. Austin, Monnett Hall, Delaware, Ohio. It states that Major Austin is buried in Grave 35, Row 33, Block F, Meuse-Argonne Cemetery at Romagne-sous-Montfaucon. Hyman Rosenberg, 28th

Top **On the flanks of Montrefagne, Hill 240, north of Exermont, the 16th Infantry work their way forward.**
(USAMHI/ASC 25040) [2/21]

Above **As incoming shellfire hits Exermont, soldiers scatter from around a Renault tank, 7 October 1918.**
(USAMHI/ASC 27424) [2/18]

Above **First Division observation post on Hill 240, 11 October.** (USAMHI/ASC 35064) [2/30]

Left **Brigadier General George C. Marshall (left), Mrs Theodore Roosevelt, Jr, Lieutenant Colonel Boswell and Lieutenant Colonel Theodore Roosevelt, Jr, 26th Infantry, at Romagne.** (USAMHI/ASC 35361) [2/34]

Infantry, who had written to his brother from Panama back in April 1917, did indeed make it to corporal. His folks had been trying to locate him and they must have been overjoyed to get a letter in February 1919 stating that there was no report of a mishap to him. In March they received another letter, saying Corporal Hyman Rosenberg had been killed in action near Véry on 12 October 1918 and had been buried at Chaudron Farm.

On the east the 33rd Division was also up for relief. They had performed the undramatic but vital task of forming a block on the Meuse, where they had stood in the mud and been shelled from the heights across the river. Chief Mechanic Andrew B. Weyer, Battery E, 122nd Field Artillery, 33rd Division, wrote home:

Well, sis, it has been just about a month since I last wrote... We are just coming out of a drive of over three weeks and I did not... have the inclination [to write] as I did not want to be one of the usual 'when they found him he had a letter in his pocket which he has not mailed'. I cheated them this time...

Right **The Meuse-Argonne American Cemetery at Romagne-sous-Montfaucon. There are 14,246 graves here and the names of 954 missing in action are inscribed on the walls of the loggias either side of the hilltop chapel.** (MFME 4/30 and 4/36)

Below **Map for the attack of the 1st Division, 9 October. Hill 272, the initial objective of the 1st Battalion, 16th Infantry, is in square F13. Hill 240 is at F11.** (USAMHI/MFME 7/23)

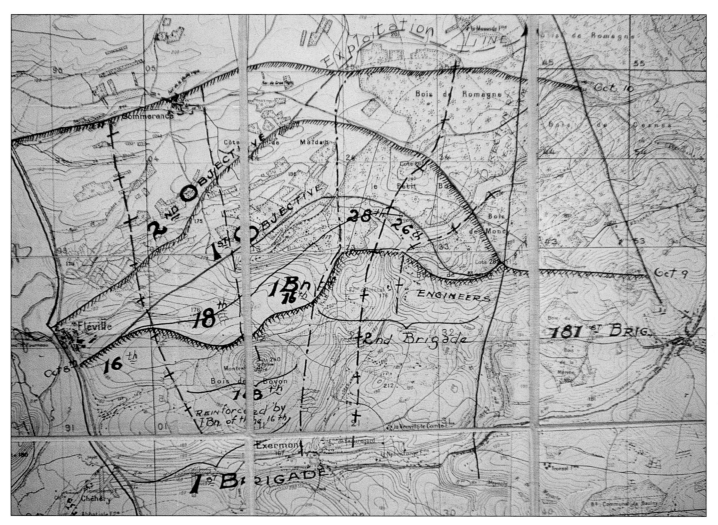

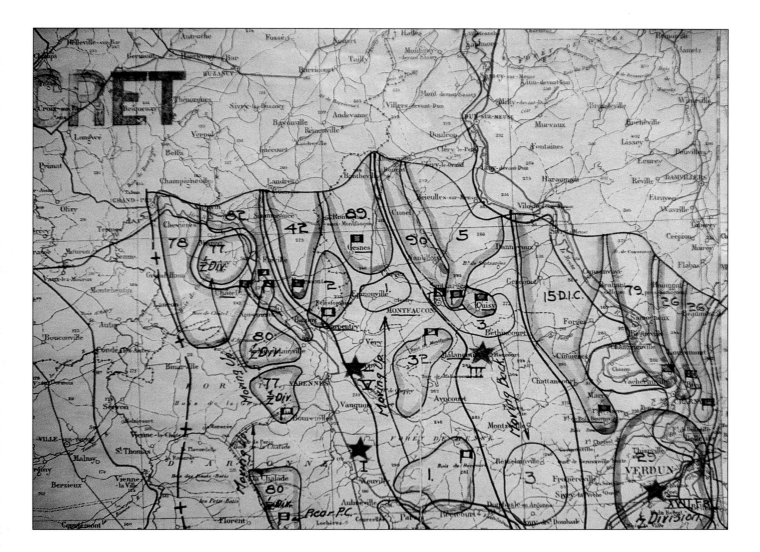

Above **The situation of the
First Army on 30 October,
1918. From the G-3 map.**
(USAMHI/MFME 7/33)

Pershing now felt it necessary to make changes amongst his commanders. Lieutenant-General George H. Cameron was relieved of V Corps and was replaced by Major-General Charles P. Summerall, until then in command of the 1st Division. Major-Generals Hunter Liggett and Robert L. Bullard moved to higher commands, Major-General Joseph T. Dickman taking over I Corps and Major-General John L. Hines III Corps. Pershing desperately needed men who could thrust the Americans forward.

Bullard assumed command of the newly formed American Second Army, which comprised the units on the St-Mihiel front and in the Vosges, while Liggett took over the First Army in the Argonne from 16 October. The divisions in the line in mid-October were of better quality than those which had started this campaign. Three regular divisions with V Corps on the right; two proven divisions, the 42nd and the 32nd, with V Corps in the centre; and the 77th and 82nd with I Corps on the left. It was in the centre, where the 42nd, 32nd and

5th faced the Romagne and Cunel Heights, that Pershing was looking for a breakthrough. The Côte Dame Marie, on the Romagne Heights west of Romagne-sous-Montfaucon, was the southernmost position of the Kriemhild Line. The line ran north-west past Hill 228 and the Côte de Châtillon, south of Landres and away west above the Aire valley. To the east it crossed the valley of the Andor, rose to the Tranchée de la Mamelle and on to the east. The 32nd Division had made some progress along the high ground of the Côte Dame Marie since 1 October. Together with the whole front line, they renewed their onslaught on 14 October, as Pershing had planned.

Together the 42nd and 32nd broke through the massive defences at last. It took three days and cost many lives. Brigadier-General Douglas MacArthur now commanded 84 Brigade, 42nd Division, and led his men from the front to take the Côte de Châtillon on 16 October. In the west, with the French making hard-won progress down the valley of the Aisne on their left flank,

Right **At Souilly, the
headquarters of the First
Army, ten miles south-west of
Verdun, Miss Anna Rochester
of the American Red Cross
feeds Sergeant W. B. Hyer,
166th Infantry.** (USAMHI/ASC
30552) [5/9]

Right **At Souilly, the
headquarters of the First
Army, ten miles south-west of
Verdun, Miss Anna Rochester
of the American Red Cross
feeds Sergeant W. B. Hyer,
166th Infantry.** (USAMHI/ASC
30552) [5/9]

Below **In the River Aire, west
of Apremont, trucks of 307th
Supply Train, 82nd Division,
and wagons of a machine-
gun battalion, 82nd Division,
and 149th Field Artillery, 42nd
Division, get cleaned up, 28
October 1918.** (USAMHI/ASC 30732)
[6/3]

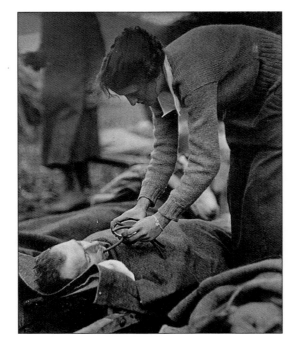

the 77th and 82nd Divisions finally achieved their goals
of Grandpré and St-Juvin to command the valley of the
Aire. In the east the town of Breulles on the Meuse was
in American hands. The greater part of the Kriemhild
Stellung had fallen and the Germans would now have to
fall back to their final line, the Freya Stellung. The
American First Army was now in the position it was
meant to have occupied by 29 September, the third day
of this campaign.

LIGGETT REGROUPS AND ATTACKS

The army General Liggett now commanded had been
badly mauled. The 42nd had lost 2,895 men killed or
wounded in the last two days. The 32nd Division was
reduced to a shadow. At a guess, perhaps 100,000
'stragglers' were adrift, separated from their units and
in a state little short of desertion. Supplies and transport were in chaos. For the next two weeks no major
attack was ordered by the allied commanders. The
exhausted divisions were relieved and the foundations
laid for a final, decisive advance.

surely have been killed; a shell went a few feet over my right shoulder and hit only a little distance behind me, it buried itself in the soft earth and only kicked mud over me... Then one of our three-inch guns began firing short and hitting in our lines and killing men... After signalling for about two hours to our artillery that they were firing short we finally had to go through the fire to reach our objective... We were in a bare slip of ground with woods on either side which was a thousand yards long. We had only gone about two hundred yards when a machine-gun opened up directly in front of us... [it] mowed the boys down... I finally spied the Germans in a trench about waist-deep, directly in front of us, but the trees behind made them hard to see.

Francis called for a Marine on his left to join in firing on the enemy, but there was no answer, for the man was dead. Another grabbed the corpse's rifle, but was immediately shot.

I kept firing and showed Arthur, who was on my right, where they were and both of us then kept on firing. Men all around us were being killed, Arthur and I being the only men alive in the front wave.

Below **An observation balloon being prepared for deployment at Cornay, 1 November. A complete telephone line system, to which the observers are being linked, has already been set up.** (USAMHI/ASC 32015) [9/34]

Left **A montage of photographs made by Earl D. Seaton of a 320-mm railroad gun.** (USAMHI/WWI/1st Div.16thInf.Seaton, Earl D.) [8/34]

As early as 29 September the German High Command was proposing an end to the war.

The enemy were in no better state. As early as 29 September the German High Command was proposing an end to the war, and Allied political and military leaders were finalising terms for an armistice.

By the end of October Liggett was ready. His artillery had been reinforced with four 14-inch naval guns mounted on railway trucks. With the help of Captain Edwin P. Hubble, a master of mathematics and astronomy, these were able to hit targets 20 miles away. (Hubble would later build the telescope at Mount Palomar, California, and it is after him that the Hubble Space Telescope is named.) Only 18 Renault light tanks were available, and these were allocated to the 2nd Division. The objective chosen by Liggett for the attack was the German line between Buzancy and Barricourt, and the 2nd and 89th Divisions were tasked with taking it. When that was done, the line along the Meuse would be pushed forward. At 3.30am on 1 November the barrage began.

Private Francis of the 5th Marines, 2nd Division, was in the line again.

...We went over at 5am, Zero hour. It had been raining and the ground was soft. I was thankful for that for I would

They held on until the company on the left out-flanked the machine-gun post and silenced it. Francis and his companion, Arthur were the sole survivors of their squad, but they made their objective late that evening. The 2nd had charged through Bayonville and the Freya Stellung beyond the village and pushed on up to the Bois de la Folie.

The 353rd Infantry, 89th Division, ran into trouble from the moment of jump-off. As they made for Rémonville they were held up time and again by machine-guns and field artillery in Bantheville Wood, but these weapons were knocked out one by one in a series of flanking attacks. They crossed the sloping, open country and took the little town and the Freya Line before turning their attention to the wooded Heights of Barricourt. By 4pm on that day, working their way forward in a series of small, murderous actions, they had taken the objective and there, as the fog started to gather and the light failed, they stopped and camped for the night.

**Below The village of
Rémonville and the woods of
Barricourt, taken by the 89th
Division, seen from the south.**
(MFME Yp/Ar 5/5)

Sergeant Rudolph A. Forderhase (as he had become), 356th Infantry, 89th Division, was following up with the reserves. He remarks:

For this operation, all NCOs, from corporal up, as well as all junior officers, had a map if able to read it or not... As we hiked through the open fields towards Rémonville... it got dark... We enjoyed a good night's sleep in Rémonville... On awakening, we found there was a fog, so dense we could hardly see across the street... As daylight came we were amazed at the labor the Germans had expended to throw barricades across the streets... almost everything moveable such as wagons, carts, furniture, bedding, and some things I was at a loss to identify. Our contemplation of the barricades was rudely interrupted by an incoming enemy artillery round, followed by many others. Considering the dense fog the accuracy of the enemy gunners could not have been better... All the shells seemed to hit the cobblestoned streets with the result that jagged fragments flew everywhere. A Corporal sitting some eight or ten feet from me took one in the neck that killed him instantly...

The next day the advance continued. Outflanked to the east, the Germans facing the 80th Division on the 2nd's left had to fall back. Enemy units further west were also forced to fall back, with resulting advances for the French Fourth Army on the other side of the forest. On 3 November the 5th Division started an outstanding three-day drive that was to take them across the Meuse on a front between Brieulles and Dun-sur-Meuse. By 5 November the American First Army had taken all the high ground and were overlooking the flood plain of the Meuse all the way from Remilly, five miles south-east of Sedan, to Sassy, just north of Dun-sur-Meuse. The Americans were ecstatic, and the French generous in their praise.

THE NORTHERN PINCER

While the American First Army was squeezing the German Army's left flank, the pressure was also being applied to the enemy's right. Having crossed the St-Quentin Canal, the British, with their American allies, were driving forward along the line of the miserable retreat of 1914. On 8 October the American 301st Heavy Tank Battalion operated with great success in support of the American II Corps and the British 6th and 25th Divisions against Brancourt, south of the Le Cateau road. On 17 October 19 of their tanks crossed the River Selle on improvised bridges to go into action. Their final action was south-east of Le Cateau on 23 October. Only the effects of gas on their accompanying infantry prevented another overwhelming success.

The 91st Division now found themselves part of the drive through southern Belgium. On 31 October they commenced an advance towards Audenarde, the Oudenarde of the Duke of Marlborough's victory of 1708, over what was thought to be a lightly defended terrain. It was not. The River Escaut (Scheldt), on which

Above **The 353rd Infantry, 89th Division, in Stenay at 10.58am, 11 November 1918.** (USAMHI/ASC 34981) [7/9]

the town stands, is a natural line of defence which the Germans were eager to hold. Bridges were destroyed and the debris partially dammed the river, causing flooding in the fields. Accurate shellfire added to the 91st's problems. On the night of 1-2 November Captain John H. Leavell, 316th Engineers, of Salt Lake City, Utah, carried out a reconnaissance in the town, which was still occupied by the Germans, to discover the exact state of the bridges and what was needed to repair them. He went back the next morning to decide where to build a bridge. He and his four men ran into an enemy patrol, but fought them off, killing five of them and capturing a Belgian who was helping the Germans. Meanwhile the 37th Division, alongside the 91st, had managed to get

across the river higher up, and their joint forces appeared to be on the brink of creating a highly exploitable bridgehead. Orders, however, came to halt, because the rest of the French Army of Belgium was not ready to advance. A new attack was planned for 10 November, but was delayed when the Germans were seen to be withdrawing in numbers, and then cancelled.

THE LAST DAYS

On 7 November rumour swept the lines – an armistice had been signed! It proved false, but it was not a frivolous invention. The Germans had cabled Marshal Foch with the names of their envoys for armistice talks to ensure the safe passage of their representatives. The

Above **The woods of the Argonne were scattered with German dead.** (USAMHI/WWI/ 1stDiv.16thInf.Kyler, Donald D.) [8/24]

Right **Supply wagons await a clear road, 9 November.** (USAMHI/ASC 44269) [2/26]

'He walked a short distance into the dark and somber woods and shot himself in the head with his service pistol.'

meeting took place on the 8th, and though the German representatives were shaken by the Allied terms they had no alternative but to accept. Meanwhile the war went on.

On the Meuse the 89th Division were now on the hills overlooking Pouilly and seeking a way across the river. The Germans, aware of the difficulties the 89th had in bringing up their artillery at the brisk pace of their advancing infantry, had managed to get most of their equipment back over the river. They had also taken or destroyed all the boats and raft-making materials. The bridges at Pouilly, hopping across the islands of firm ground in the marshy flood plain, appeared to be intact and were reported as such. In this report, however, Captain Arthur Y. Wear, 3rd Battalion, 356th Infantry, was mistaken, for the last arch of the bridge closest to the town was badly damaged and the bridge over the canal was gone. They had to find a way across the river. Accounts of what followed vary. The divisional history and the reports of a man who was there do not tally in detail, but the broad account of events seems clear.

Sergeant Forderhase tells it this way.

Captain Arthur Y. Wear was now in command of the battalion. He had orders to get men across the river. He now called for men to volunteer to swim across the river and attempt to get information as to the strength and disposition of the German troops. The stream was near bankfull... the water was cold and deep. Only about half of those who volunteered were selected. Of these, only a few succeeded in getting across. About half were killed by the enemy or drowned in the cold water. Only about half of those who got back were able to give information of any value. The Battalion moved to the top of the hill to wait for daylight... When the surviving swimmers returned and informed Captain Wear of what had been accomplished, he walked a short distance into the dark and somber woods and shot himself in the head with his service pistol.

Wear had only recently returned to his regiment from after recovering in hospital. Forderhase was sympathetic to him, and angry at commanders in the rear who had put pressure on him to demand such a sacrifice from his men.

While the problem of crossing the river was studied by the engineers, the 356th sat tight. In the early hours of 9 November, Forderhase was in command of a squad guarding the approaches to the bridge. In the heavy fog they heard a sound like people wading through the shallow waters by the canal. They went on the alert. Then they heard a grunt and a squeal – wild pigs! The temptation to add the hogs to their field rations was resisted.

On 10 November the engineers produced the answer to the crossing problem. They had managed to bring up pontoons and float them in a little tributary to the Meuse. That night the 356th Infantry were ferried over. Cautiously, Forderhase's squad advanced through the fog which again shrouded the land.

Captain Ernsberger did not see the two young Germans, with their light machine-gun, until he was close up to them. They were standing in a shallow pit they had dug with their hands held high in surrender. I could not see the incident, but the Captain called me to come. I was quite surprised to see them. The Captain knew I could speak a bit of German and told me to ask them why they had not fired on us. They informed me that all fighting was to end at eleven o'clock that morning and they saw no reason to sacrifice their lives, or ours, needlessly. Neither the Captain, nor I, knew whether to believe them or not.

On the right flank of the 356th, Captain F. M. Wood, 353rd Infantry, 89th Division, had been advancing towards the Meuse at Stenay.

Swampy ground saved us a great many casualties as the shells penetrated to a considerable depth before exploding. A large shell hit in front of a funk hole occupied by Sgt H. O. Bull and Pvt S. C. Toby... exploding directly under them, raising the ground up but not breaking through. Sgt Bull said: 'What are they trying to do now?' then turned over and went back to sleep.

Nov. 10, we were ordered forward to relieve the 355th Inf... In retreating behind the Meuse the enemy had dammed a small tributary; flooded the entire lowlands making the crossing of the Meuse a most difficult problem. However, by heroic work Lt Connors of A Company led his platoon across the morning of Nov. 11th...

Far to the left of the 89th, outside Sedan, a chaotic situation had just been resolved. Shortly after noon on 6 November General Summerall, commanding V Corps,

arrived at 1st Division headquarters and handed Brigadier-General Frank Parker a message purporting to be from General Liggett, the First Army commander. It was addressed to the commanding generals, I and V Corps, and stated that General Pershing 'desires [that] the honour of entering Sedan should fall to the First American Army'. It went on to say that the C-in-C was confident that I Corps, assisted by V Corps on their right, would enable him to realise this desire, and con-

cluded with the words: 'Boundaries will not be considered binding.' It was a formula for confusion. The 1st Division was then set in motion to turn left and head for Sedan, seven miles from its own sector, passing through the I Corps area, across the fronts of the 77th and 42nd Divisions. Parker sent liaison officers to I Corps HQ (arriving at 9pm) and to the 6th Division (arriving at 6.30pm) which, according to the divisional history, was to the 1st Division's immediate left. Other

sources put the 77th there. Five columns moved off between 7pm and 8pm to make a night march on, perforce, the roads.

Private Herbert L. McHenry's Machine-Gun Company, 16th Infantry, was in Column 1.

We were a whole nights hike from Sedan. We were informed the Col. Ryder would lead our Battalion up the Meuse River Road to Sedan... The night was dark and misty, and we were under enemy fire the whole trip... The German Army was on retreat and was burning all supplies it could not take with it... The Germans had mined the road and destroyed all the bridges. I may be mixed [up] on this, but we seemed to be marching through the rear guard of the retreating German Army... As we passed along we could see Germans, not more than 30 feet to our right firing flare pistols... as soon as the flare died down we moved swiftly ahead... [they] were picking our men off as we marched along, but we did not open an engagement with them but moved on. The hardest thing... was the cry of the wounded as they pleaded with us not to leave them there...

The wild march continued through the night. At daybreak McHenry and his companions found themselves in a town strongly held by the Germans, probably Pont Maugis. His squad became separated from the rest and took cover in a large garden, staying there for four hours before being found and given the location of the rest of the 16th. That night, 7-8 November, they slept and in the morning they ran across an advance post of the 42nd Division. The rest of the day they stayed under cover, eventually withdrawing when they discovered that the 1st Division had been withdrawn on the afternoon of 7 November. Liggett had found out what was being done in his name and countermanded the order. McHenry was convinced that the town they had under their guns on that last day was Sedan.

The experiences of the other 1st Division columns were equally arduous and confusing. One unit actually captured Brigadier-General Douglas MacArthur of the 42nd, thinking him a spy. The wrongly attributed order and the subsequent march on Sedan made a curious episode, from which the commanders deserved no credit — only the men distinguished themselves.

ARMISTICE

The Germans signed the terms of the armistice at Compiègne at 5.10am on 11 November. Hostilities were to cease at 11am that day. The news was sent as swiftly as possible to all units, but failed to reach many of them in time. In some formations there seemed to

Left **The 105th Field Artillery, 27th Division, celebrate the Armistice at Etraye, west of Damvillers, 11 November.**
(USAMHI/ASC 33075) [7/2]

I took a look at the cheap wristwatch. It had stopped at eleven o'clock and I never did get it to run again. It was past 11.30am when we got orders to cease firing.

be little desire to end the war, and attacks were planned and executed up to and in some cases even beyond the stated time.

The men of the 356th Infantry, including Sergeant Forderhase, made their way forward to the high ground beyond Pouilly in the thinning fog.

We had come up to a terrace wall of stone. We had come upon a small group of Germans armed with two machine-guns, and an officer armed with a rifle. I took a few steps to my left and came upon the scene just as one of our corporals fired at, and killed, the young German officer. He had killed two of our riflemen before he himself fell... One of our runners had been severely wounded... A sniper, located somewhere above us in the forest, was firing on our troops in the village below us. Apparently he could not see us and we could not see him. We were somewhat concerned about this when suddenly the sniper's firing ceased – everything became perfectly quiet. I then remembered what the two German prisoners had said earlier that morning. I took a look at the cheap wristwatch that I had been wearing. It had stopped at eleven o'clock and I never did get it to run again. It was past 11.30am when we got orders to cease firing.

On the eastern side of the Meuse, in the Verdun Forest north of Douaumont, the 26th Division was still improving its position. Corporal Harry G. Wright of the 104th Infantry was there:

On the Monday, Nov. 11 1918, we had orders to go over and push [the Germans] over a hill that was in front of us. We were froze, tired and hungry as the Zero hour approached. But just before we started our last drive which would have meant many more lives, an order came through to cease firing. An armistice had been signed for 11 o'clock and it is now 10.30. One half [hour] more of this hell on earth with us on the verge of going over the top again. How our artillery was pounding behind us. Just waiting for 11 o'clock and us doughboys were moving slowly toward the hill just as tho' we new nothing about it or what it meant. But now it is 11 o'clock Nov. 11 1918 and all our guns stopped and we stopped in our tracks and hugged each other and

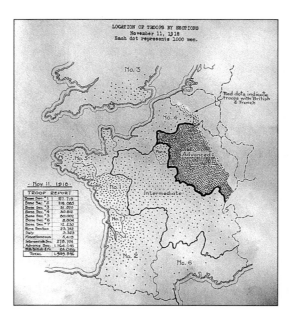

Above **The location of troops at 11 November 1918.**
(USAMHI/Rpt Com. Gen. SOS, May 1919) [7/37]

Right **Lieutenant-Colonel Patch and Major Allen of the 18th Infantry, 1st Division, cross the border into Lorraine, 20 November.** (USAMHI/ASC 35064) [2/31]

danced to keep warm and what a celebration was going on across the line on the Germans' side. They were shooting rockets and flares and hollering and dancing in glee.

On the Woevre Plain the French II Colonial Corps had been making for the town of Metz, supported by the American 129th Field Artillery. Captain Harry S. Truman recalled:

... I was to say nothing about the cessation of hostilities until 11am. My battery fired the assigned barrages at the times specified. The last one toward a tiny village called Hermeville eleven thousand meters from my position. My last shot was fired at 10.45. When the firing ceased all along the front lines it seemed not so. It was so quiet it made me feel as if I'd suddenly been deprived of my ability to hear.

In the Meuse-Argonne offensive the Americans had lost 117,000 men killed, wounded, missing or taken prisoner. In the war as a whole they had sustained losses of 278,983, of whom 48,909 were killed and 9,294 made prisoner. John J. Pershing had created a 20th-century army. The Allies had won the war. The United States had taken her place as a champion of democratic freedom on the world stage. Yet the failure to win the peace or to lend strength to its protection would mean that Americans would fight again over this ground in years to come.

BIBLIOGRAPHY

The literature of the First World War is extensive. The list given here is of those works the author has consulted in the preparation of this book and is therefore partial and personal. The books from which quotations are taken are included.

American Armies and Battlefields in Europe, Washington, DC, Center of Military History, United States Army/US Government Printing Office, 1938, reprinted 1992.

Americans in the Great War, The:
Volume 1, *The Second Battle of the Marne,* Clermont-Ferrand, Michelin, 1919.
Volume 2, *The Battle of Saint-Mihiel,* Clermont-Ferrand, Michelin, 1919.
Volume 3, *Meuse-Argonne Battle,* Clermont-Ferrand, Michelin, 1919.

Brittain, Vera, *Testament of Youth,* London, Victor Gollancz, 1933.

Coombs, Rose (ed. Karel Margry), *Before Endeavours Fade: A Guide to the Battlefields of the First World War,* London, Battle of Britain Prints International, 1994.

Evarts, Jeremiah, *Cantigny: A Corner of the War,* USA, privately printed, 1938.

Fletcher, David (ed.), *Tanks and Trenches,* Stroud, Sutton Publishing, 1994.

Gilbert, Martin, *First World War,* London, Weidenfeld & Nicolson, 1994.

Gray, Randal, with Christopher Argyle, *Chronicle of the First World War,* Volume II, *1917-1921,* Oxford and New York, Facts on File, 1991.

Griess, Thomas (ed.), *The Great War,* The West Point Military History Series, Wayne, NJ, Avery Publishing Group, 1986.

Harbord, James G., *Report of the Commanding General, Services of Supply, to the Commander in Chief,* typescript, May 1919.

Harries, Meirion and Susie, *The Last Days of Innocence: America at War, 1917-1918,* New York, Random House, 1997.

Hendrick, Burton, *The Life and Letters of Walter H. Page,* 3 Volumes, London, William Heinemann, 1922 and 1926.

History of the First Division During the World War 1917-1919, Philadelphia, PA, John C. Winston, 1931.

History of the 89th Division, USA, Denver, CO, War Society of the 89th Division, 1920.

Johnson, Hubert, *Breakthrough!,* Novato, CA, Presidio Press, 1994.

Judy, Will, *A Soldier's Diary,* Chicago, IL, Judy Publishing, 1930.

Lawson, Eric and Jane, *The First Air Campaign,* Conshohocken, PA, Combined Books, 1996.

Livesey, Anthony, *The Viking Atlas of World War I,* London and New York, Penguin Books, 1994.

McHenry, Herbert, *As a Private Saw It,* Indiana, PA, A. G. Halldin Publishing, 1988.

Macksey, Kenneth, and William Woodhouse, *The Penguin Encyclopedia of Modern Warfare,* London and New York, Viking, 1991.

Mendenhall, John, 'The Fist in the Dyke', *Infantry Journal,* January/February 1936.

Patton, Robert, *The Pattons, A Personal History of an American Family,* Washington, DC, and London, Brassey's, 1994.

Pershing, John J., *My Experiences in the World War,* London, Hodder & Stoughton, 1931.

Second Division, American Expeditionary Force, in France, 1917-1919, The, New York, The Hillman Press, 1937.

Smythe, Donald, *Pershing: General of the Armies,* Bloomington, IN, Indiana University Press, 1986.

Stallings, Laurence, *The Doughboys: The Story of the AEF 1917-1918,* New York, Harper & Row, 1963.

Story of the 91st Division, The, San Francisco, 91st Division Publication Committee, 1919.

Terraine, John, *To Win a War: 1918, The Year of Victory,* London, Macmillan, 1986.

Thomason, John W., Jr, *Fix Bayonets! – With the US Marine Corps in France 1917-1918,* New York, Charles Scribner's Sons, 1925; reprinted London, Greenhill Books, 1989.

Tuchman, Barbara, *August 1914,* London, Constable, 1962; entitled *The Guns of August* in the USA.

Warrum, Noble, *Utah in the World War,* Salt Lake City, UT, 1924.

Weintraub, Stanley, *A Stillness Heard Round the World,* New York, E. P. Dutton and London, Allen & Unwin, 1985.

Williams, Ralph, *The Luck of a Buck,* Madison, WI, Fitchburg Press, 1985.

Windrow, Martin, and Gerry Embleton, *Military Dress of North America,* London, Ian Allan, 1973.

Wise, Jennings, *The Turn of the Tide,* New York, Henry Holt and Company, 1920.

Below **The American Battle Monuments Commission Aisne-Marne Cemetery at Belleau Wood contains the graves of 2,289 men. The chapel walls carry the names of 1,060 missing.** (MFME Yp/Ar 7/1)

INDEX

The American Somme Cemetery, Bevy

In their devotion, their valor, and in the loyal
fulfillment of their obligations, the officers
and men of the American Expeditionary Forces
have left a heritage of which those who follow
may be proud.

General John J. Pershing